TWAYNE'S WORLD AUTHORS SERIES

A Survey of the World's Literature

Sylvia E. Bowman, Indiana University
GENERAL EDITOR

FRANCE

Maxwell A. Smith, Guerry Professor of French, Emeritus
The University of Chattanooga
Former Visiting Professor in Modern Languages
The Florida State University

EDITOR

Georges Simenon

TWAS 456

Georges Simenon

GEORGES SIMENON

By LUCILLE FRACKMAN BECKER

Drew University

TWAYNE PUBLISHERS

A DIVISION OF G. K. HALL & CO., BOSTON

Library of Congress Cataloging in Publication Data

Becker, Lucille Frackman.
    Georges Simenon.

    (Twayne's world authors series ; TWAS 456. France)
    Bibliography: p. 153 - 65.
    Includes index.
1.   Simenon, Georges, 1903 -   —Criticism and interpreta-
tion.
PQ2637.I53Z58   843'.9'12   77-2577
ISBN 0-8057-6293-0

Contents

About the Author

Professor Lucille Becker is Chairperson of the French Department at Drew University, Madison, N.J. She received the B.A. degree from Barnard College, a Diplôme d'Etudes Françaises from the University of Aix-Marseilles where she studied under a Fulbright Grant, and her M.A. and Ph.D. from Columbia University. Her articles and reviews have appeared in *The Nation, Colliers Encyclopedia, Yale French Studies, Romanic Review, French Review, Modern Language Journal, Romance Notes,* and *Books Abroad.* She contributed a chapter to the book *Montherlant vu par des jeunes de 17 à 27 ans* and edited a critical text of Montherlant's play *Le Maître de Santiago.* Her most recent books include *Henry de Montherlant, A Critical Biography* and *Louis Aragon,* which was published in Twayne's World Authors Series. Dr. Becker is a member of Phi Beta Kappa.

Preface

Georges Simenon's productivity has been a source of amazement to critics and has often diverted them from a consideration of the literary merits of his work. Since writing his first novel, *Au Pont des Arches*, at the age of sixteen, he has published more than two hundred potboilers under seventeen pseudonyms, 102 novels and short stories devoted to the cases of Commissaire Maigret, 114 additional short stories, 116 novels, thirteen autobiographical works, thirty series of articles, and a ballet scenario. Simenon's work has been translated into forty languages, and estimates have been made that over fifty million copies of his novels have been published. More than fifty-five movies have been made from his novels, six of them were adapted for the theater, and several television series have been built around Maigret.

Even more remarkable than the quantity of Simenon's work is its generally superior quality. His novels are marked by an extraordinary blend of narrative skill and psychological insight. His incisive probing into the tragedy of human existence caused François Mauriac to characterize his work as a "nightmare described with unbearable artistry."[1]

Drawing heavily from Simenon's works in an effort to present him as much as possible in his own words, I have traced the origin of his major themes and characters in the autobiographical works *Je me souviens* and *Pedigree*. Proceeding to the novels, I then examined the "Maigrets," the novels devoted to Simenon's legendary policeman who has been immortalized in bronze in the city of Delfzijl where Simenon created him, showing how Simenon transformed the rules and techniques of the detective novel and used it, as he did his other novels, to express the most important themes of the twentieth century: guilt and innocence, alienation and solitude. The major part of the study is devoted to an analysis of the basic themes in Simenon's work as they appear and reappear, with infinite variations and subtle modifications.

In the final chapter, I have analyzed Simenon's theories on the art of the novel and the role of the novelist, as well as his application of the rules of Greek tragedy to the novel, which is, for him, the tragic medium of our time. In discussing Simenon's style, I have attempted to analyze the atmosphere, or what he terms the "poetic line," of his novels, which according to one critic contain more poetry than most books that pretend to contain poetry because they are printed in irregular lines.[2]

It would be impossible to deal with Simenon's vast literary production within the scope offered by the present study. I have, however, discussed the essential elements of his art, illustrating my observations with selections chosen according to my preferences and emphasizing works like *Le Grand Bob, Le Clan des Ostendais, La Mort d'Auguste, La Fuite de Monsieur Monde, L'Enterrement de Monsieur Bouvet, Les Anneaux de Bicêtre, L'Horloger d'Everton, Les Volets verts, Le Petit Saint*, while omitting, by necessity, the discussion of other excellent novels. The novels chosen, however, suffice to demonstrate why André Gide called Georges Simenon the greatest modern French novelist.

Acknowledgment

I am particularly grateful to Georges Simenon for his kind and generous permission to quote from his works.

Chronology

(Titles and dates of first publication of Simenon's more than 250 works are included in the chronological bibliography at the end of the book. This chronology includes facts about his life and the number of volumes written each year.)

1903 Georges Joseph Christian Simenon born in Liége, February 13.

1906 Birth of Christian Simenon, Georges's brother.

1907 Simenon family moves to rue de la Loi, where Henriette Simenon begins to take in foreign students as boarders.

1909 Enters Institut Saint-André.

1914 Enters collège Saint-Louis as a scholarship student.

1915 Leaves collège Saint-Louis for collège Saint-Servais. Family moves again, to rue des Maraîchers.

1918 Family moves to rue de l'Enseignement. Doctor informs Simenon that his father is seriously ill. Simenon leaves school to be apprenticed to a pastry cook. Shortly afterward, he becomes a salesclerk in Librairie Georges and is fired after six weeks.

1919 Cub reporter on Gazette de Liége. Given his own column, "From the Hen Roost," which he signs Monsieur le Coq. Frequents a group of young painters and poets calling themselves "la Caque" who meet in a ruined house behind the Saint-Pholien Church. Writes his first novel, *Au Pont des Arches*.

1920 Engaged to Régine Renchon. Enlists in army to finish military service as early as possible. Spends eighteen months in service near his home and continues to write for Gazette de Liége. Désiré Simenon dies.

1922 Goes to Paris. Becomes secretary to Binet-Valmer, chairman of Ligue des Chefs de Section et Anciens Combattants.

1923 Marriage to Régine Renchon in Liége on March 24. Returns to Paris and begins to write short stories for *Le Matin* and other Parisian newspapers. Writes over one thousand of these stories in the next ten years. Secretary to Marquis de Tracy, travels with him to many of his châteaux.

1924   Leaves service of Marquis de Tracy; settles in Paris where he begins to write potboilers, the first of which, *Le Roman d'un dactylo*, was written in one morning on the terrace of a cafe.

1925   Writes two hundred fourteen potboilers under seventeen pseudonyms from 1925 to 1934. Summer in Porquerolles.

1928   Buys his first boat, the *Ginette*, and spends the summer touring the rivers and canals of France.

1929   Has larger boat, *l'Ostrogoth*, built, on which he travels as far as Delfzijl in Holland. Travels to Norway and Lapland by regular boat. Returns to Delfzijl where he writes first Maigret, *Pietr-le-Letton*, in September. Writes short stories for *Detective: Les 13 Mystères, Les 13 Enigmes, Les 13 Coupables*.

1930   Writes thirteen novels. February — Launches Maigret series by an "anthropometric dance" at the Boule Blanche in Montparnasse. Jean Renoir buys film rights to *La Nuit du carrefour* and Abel Tarride to *Le Chien jaune*.

1931   Articles, *Escales nordiques*, published in *Le Petit Journal*, March 1-21, 1931. Articles, *L'Aventure entre deux berges*, published in *Vu*, July 1, 1931.

1932   Article, *Au Fil de l'eau*, in *Le Figaro illustré*, May 1, 1932. Articles, *L'Heure du Negre*, in *Voilà*, Nos. 81 - 86, October 8 - November 12, 1932. Writes thirteen novels. *La Tête d'un homme* adapted for the cinema. Buys property, La Richardière, in Marsilly near La Rochelle where his first wife still lives.

1933   Writes five novels. Tours Europe in summer and writes series of articles, *Peuples qui ont faim (Hungry People)*. Publishes articles in *Voilà, Police et Reportage, Détective, Témoignages de notre temps*. Publishes articles, *Chez Trotsky*, about his visit with Trotsky, in *Paris-Soir*, June 16 and 17, 1933.

1934   Writes four novels. Articles, *Peuples qui ont faim*, published in *Le Jour*, April-May 1934. Articles, *En Marge de l'affaire Stavisky*, reports on the Stavisky affair, published in *Paris-Soir*, January-February 1934.
Articles, *A la recherche des assassins du conseiller Prince*, *Paris-Soir*, March-April 1934. Articles in *Excelsior, Je Sais Tout, Le Jour*. Rents a schooner, the *Araldo*, on which he tours the Mediterranean during the summer. Articles on this trip, *Mare Nostrum*, published in *Vu*. Sued by a hotel keeper in Libreville for defamation in *Le Coup de lune*.

1935   Writes three novels. Travels around the world: New York, Panama, Colombia, the Equator, the Galapagos, Tahiti, New Zealand, Australia, the Indies, the Red Sea. Articles on his travels in Central America, *En marge des méridiens*, published in *Marianne*. Series of articles on his travels, *Les Vaincus de l'aventure*, published in *Paris-Soir*, June 12 - 25, 1935. Published by Gallimard in 1938, entitled *La Mauvaise étoile*. Additional articles published in *Le Jour* and *Paris-Soir*.

1936   Writes seven novels. Sued for *Quartier Nègre*.

1937   Writes seven novels. Articles, *Police Secours* or *les Nouveaux Mystères de Paris*, published in *Paris-Soir*, February 6 - 16, 1937. Articles, *Long cours sur les rivières et canaux*, in *Marianne*, later published under same title by Editions Dynamo, Liége, 1952.

1938   Four novels. Three collections of short stories: *Le Petit Docteur, Les Dossiers de l'Agence O, Les Nouvelles Enquêtes de Maigret*.

1939   Six novels. Birth of his son Marc.

1940   Three novels. Organizes aid to refugees at La Rochelle. A radiologist incorrectly reads his x-rays and tells him that he has less than two years to live. Settles in château de Terre-Neuve at Fontenay-le-Comte.

1941   Four novels.

1942   Writes autobiographical work, *Je me souviens*. One novel. Starts transforming *Je me souviens* into autobiographical novel, *Pedigree*.

1943   Completes *Pedigree*. Two novels.

1944   Two novels. Short stories, *Le Bateau d'Emile*.

1945   Three novels. Travels to Montreal and New York. Meets Denise Ouimet who will become his second wife. Articles, *Au chevet du monde malade*, in *France-Soir*.

1946   Five novels. Articles on Canada for *France-Soir*, *Le Canada*. Travels to Florida, Alabama, Tennessee, Georgia. Articles on travels through the United States, *l'Amérique en voiture*, for *France-Soir*.

1947   Five novels. Short stories of *Maigret et les petits cochons sans queue*. Travels to Cuba, crosses desert by car and settles in Arizona.

1948   Four novels.

1949   Six novels. Birth of his second son, Johnny, to Denise Ouimet. Settles in California.

1950   Seven novels. Divorced from Régine Renchon at Reno, marries Denise. Settles at Shadow Rock Farm, Lakeville, Connecticut.

1951   Six novels.

1952   Four novels. Returns to Belgium where he is elected to the Belgian Royal Academy of Language and Literature. Sued in Belgium for *Pedigree;* loses suit and decides to forego writing future volumes. Travels to Paris, Milan, Rome, Brussels, Liége. Returns to Lakeville.

1953   Six novels. Birth of Simenon's daughter, Marie-Georges.

1954   Five novels.

1955   Five novels. Returns to Europe with his family.

1956   Four novels.

1957   Five novels. Settles with family at Echandens, near Lausanne.

1958   Three novels. Delivers speech, *Le Roman de l'homme,* at Brussels Exposition Universelle. Presides over Brussels Film Festival.

1959   Four novels. Birth of son Pierre.

1960   Three novels. Presides at Cannes Film Festival.

1961   Four novels.

1962   Four novels. Moves to mansion at Epalinges near Lausanne, his twenty-ninth home.

1963   Denise leaves for sanatorium after nervous breakdown and never returns to Epalinges. Simenon remains with three youngest children and Theresa, his companion. Three novels.

1964   Two novels.

1965   Three novels.

1966   Four novels. Bronze statue of Maigret erected at Delfzijl.

1967   Three novels.

1968   Four novels.

1969   Three novels.

1970   Three novels.

1971   Four novels.

1972   One novel. Sells Epalinges; moves to apartment in Lausanne.

1973   Decides to stop writing novels, starts dictating into tape recorder; from September 1973 to the end of March 1974 dictates three texts: *Lettre à ma mère* (published in 1974); *Des Traces de pas, Un Homme comme un autre* (1975) Buys a small eighteenth century house next door to apartment house in Lausanne. Doctorat honoris causa from University of Liége.

1974 Moves into small house.

1976 Publishes two additional volumes of dictated reflections: *Les Petits hommes* and *Vent du nord-Vent du sud.*

.

CHAPTER 1

Pedigree

I *Portrait of a City, a Class, and a Family*

"   "IN those humble surroundings in which he spent his childhood, there was a child-spy . . . who collected, recorded, retained, without realizing it, everyday life in its obscure complexity."[1] Mauriac's description of his childhood parallels Simenon's observation that he has always retained a stereoscopic memory of his first twenty years and is able to reconstruct even the most trifling events in their precise chronological order.[2] For Simenon, this period is the most important in a man's life. "I think that man only absorbs substance, only grows until he is about eighteen years old. What you have not absorbed at eighteen, you will no longer absorb. It's over. You will be able to develop what you have absorbed. You will be able to make something of it or nothing at all. You have finished the period of absorption and, the rest of your life, you will remain, in consequence, the slave of your childhood and early adolescence."[3]

Simenon's autobiographical works, the record of his childhood and adolescence, contain the themes and characters of his novels. What he has done, explains André Parinaud, is to use his prodigious memory as an encyclopedia, borrowing from it a name, a tic, a gesture, an atmosphere. Using this as a starting point, he goes beyond it, integrating it into a new reality, which is the novel.[4]

When Simenon, at the age of thirty-eight, was told by a doctor who had misread his chest x-rays that he had less than two years to live, he decided to write the story of his childhood in the form of a letter addressed to his two year old son, Marc. He felt that this was the only way in which his son would ever have a chance to know about his father and his father's family. When Simenon sent the first hundred pages to André Gide, Gide advised him to rewrite the work in the third person in the form of a novel. The original autobiographical pages of *Je me souviens (I Remember)* were incorporated into the first part of the novel *Pedigree*. In the preface to *Pedigree*, Simenon wrote:

The childhood of Roger Mamelin, his milieu, the setting in which he develops, are very close to reality, as are the people he observed. The events, for the most part, are not invented. But, above all, as far as the characters are concerned, I exercised the writer's privilege of recreating reality, starting from composite material; remaining closer to poetic truth than to pure and simple truth. . . . *Pedigree* is a novel, thus a work in which imagination and recreation play the greatest role, but this does not prevent me from admitting that Roger Mamelin has a great deal in common with the child I once was.[5]

In the novel, Simenon presents by a series of flashbacks a portrait of a city, a class, and a family during the early years of the twentieth century. The lives of the characters are played out against the background of the major political and social events of the time; the Agadir crisis, anarchist bombings, general strikes, the German occupation, the armistice, the English pit disaster at Souverain-Wandre, and the echoes of revolutionary intrigue brought to Liége by impoverished students from Eastern Europe. These events, however, are important only as they affect the characters in the novel.

II *Liége*

Simenon recreates the whole sensory world of his childhood as he evokes the sounds, sights, and smells of the city of Liége with its houses, streets, canals, barges, the different seasons and changes of climate. He is particularly interested in the familiar, imprecise, fragmentary aspects of the city, "sidewalks in the rain, the rumbling of the streetcars which jolt in the street, dawn over the market places, the appearance of 'bouquettes' [Liégois crêpes] on Christmas eve and the warm wine to accompany them, the horse-drawn barges, fog over the canals, the wagons filled with vegetables, and the cries of the tradeswomen, the flowers in the open air stalls . . . the alleys filled with the smell of French fried potatoes, the casseroles of mussels, and the large glasses of beer . . . the odor of gin, of tar, of ginger, of leeks and cloves."[6]

He describes, too, the families dressed in their Sunday best to visit their relatives after church, and the holidays that periodically interrupt the daily routine:

The breath of the city is laden with smells that are characteristic of the days which preceed the Feast of Saint Nicolas. Although it is not yet snowing, invisible specks of ice float in space like dust and pile up in the luminous halos of the shop windows.

Everyone is out of doors. All the women run, dragging behind them children who would like to stop longer in front of the displays. . . . The confectioners' shops, the pastry shops, the grocery stores are swarming with people. . . . Two smells dominate the others, so characteristic that no child could mistake them, the sweet, fragrant odor of gingerbread and that of chocolate figurines, which is not the same smell as the smell of chocolate bars. From top to bottom, the store windows are piled up with honey cakes, some of them stuffed with multicolored, preserved fruits. Life-size gingerbread figures of Saint Nicolas stand with cotton wool beards, surrounded by sheep, donkeys, barnyard animals, all brownish colored or the color of whole wheat bread, sugared, perfumed, edible. It makes one's head swim. . . . December with Saint Nicolas's day, then Christmas, then the New Year, is a month heavy with mystery, of sweet, somewhat troubling impressions which follow one another in a breathless rhythm.

The students are feverish. Night falls and the snowflakes become thicker, slower. . . . They open their mouths, put out their tongues, they try to catch a snowflake which has a faint taste of dust. They affirm with conviction: "It is good." And it is good, in fact, the first cold spell, the first snowfall, a world that has lost its daily appearance, roofs which are blurred against the dull sky, lights which scarcely illuminate any longer and passersby who float in space. Even the streetcar becomes a mysterious vessel, with windows for portholes.[7]

III   *Petite Bourgeoisie*

Using Liége as a setting, whether busy with its daily peacetime pursuits or occupied by the Germans, torn by strikes and riots or caught up in the magic of the Exposition Universelle, Simenon describes the life of a class, the petite bourgeoisie, blindly struggling against its mediocrity. Despite their modest economic situation, Simenon's parents, who belonged to this class, considered themselves superior to the working class and the peasantry. Simenon describes this attitude in *Je me souviens* as he reminisces about trips to market with his mother. She would drag him quickly past the inns where, in the dark interior, he saw peasants eating enormous plates of bacon and eggs and slices of bread as large and thick as wagon wheels. For years, Simenon recalls, he was hungry for this "peasant food," which his mother scorned as she "slipped through this enchanted world, dignified, constantly counting, an eager child hanging on to her skirts."[8]

In the same work, Simenon admonishes his son never to forget these humble origins. "You live in a château, you have a park at your disposal . . . a distinguished governess follows your every step . . . I clutch hold of the fragile chain which links you to those from whom you are descended, the little world of little people who struggled in their turn—as tomorrow you will in yours—confusedly seeking a means of escape, a goal, a raison d'être, an explanation for good luck or misfortune, a hope for an improved condition and for serenity."[9]

Much later, in his *Lettre à ma mère*, written to his mother after her death, Simenon stated: "All your life, you insisted on belonging to the world of people of small means. It would greatly astonish you to learn that, at my age, I draw nearer to it because I feel that it is my world also and because it is the world of truth."[10] All of Simenon's work expresses this sympathy for the little man.

The world of the petite bourgeoisie was that of practicing Catholics, and the festivals and holidays Simenon describes are religious in nature. In *Pedigree*, he conveys Roger's joy as his first communion approaches and his disillusionment when he finds that it has not transformed him as he anticipated. Roger, like Simenon, was an altar boy, and the atmosphere of Sundays in his parish would mark him forever. In Simenon's work, there are continual references to this Catholic atmosphere, allusions to church buildings and liturgy, images borrowed from religion, where clouds look like angels, rooms smell like sacristies, and women are as cold as theological virtues.[11] In an article entitled "Simenon et l'enfant de choeur" ("Simenon and the altar boy"), Marcel Moré traces the use of these references throughout Simenon's work and mentions that, at a higher level, the anguish of many of Simenon's characters is merely their awareness that they exist in a world deprived of divine grace.[12] Nonetheless, religious questions are as absent from Simenon's work, as are political considerations. Religion, Simenon maintains, is a question that is too personal, too intimate, to be dealt with in a novel.[13]

IV *Henriette Simenon (Elise)*

In *Pedigree*, Simenon presents an unforgettable portrait of his mother, the dominant influence on his life and work. Henriette

Brüll (Elise in *Pedigree*) was of mixed German and Dutch parentage, the youngest of thirteen children "whom nobody had expected, and who had turned up to complicate everything."[14] Her father had occupied the prestigious post of dike master in Holland before his alcoholism brought ruin upon him and his family. In *Je me souviens*, Simenon tells his son: "When you know Holland, the Low Countries, the polders, you will understand that it [dike master] is a sort of nobility and perhaps one of the most beautiful."[15] His mother's life "as a frightened unhappy little mouse had begun when she was five, when her father had died and the family had left the huge house by the canal at Herstal."[16] She and her mother, from whom she inherited her inordinate pride, came to Liége. In order to camouflage their poverty, Elise's mother would put empty saucepans on the stove when visitors arrived. When her mother died, she became a domestic in the home of one of her wealthy, married sisters, left her sister's home to become a salesgirl in the Innovation department store, and then left this position to marry Désiré Simenon.

Elise's background explains her dreadful fear of poverty and her insatiable need for security. Simenon portrays his mother as the most tormented of individuals, subject to nervous crises and gratuitous crying fits. "She suffers because of everything . . . she suffers through habit."[17] She feels instinctively that something dreadful is always about to happen. She has an abnormal fear of finding herself without means once again and harbors a grudge against Désiré for being happy in his life and work and for accepting life as it is. His calm contentment exasperates her. She seems almost to take morbid pleasure in her own anguish. In *Les Quatre jours du pauvre homme*, Simenon lends his mother's temperament to the protagonist's mother: "How she loved misfortunes! She would have knit them! She would have begged God to make them rain down on our heads."[18] Simenon is able to transmit in his novels this continual dread of impending catastrophe.

Elise's humble manner and constant complaints hide an iron will that will let nothing stand in the way of her desire for security. Soon after Roger's birth, Elise asks Désiré to take out a life insurance policy. She is furious when he shrugs off her request, not knowing that he had applied and been turned down because of the heart condition that was to cause his death at the age of forty-three. She then decides that she will insure her security herself and moves her family to a house on the rue de la Loi which she converts into a boarding house for foreign students. Years later, driven by the same urge for security, she would marry a government employee whose benefits included a widow's pension.

His mother's second marriage inspired Simenon's novel *Le Chat*. Very soon after their marriage, Simenon's mother and her second husband began to distrust one another. He accused her, not entirely without reason, of being in a hurry to collect her widow's pension. Together, in the large house without boarders, Simenon wrote,

the sentences you exchanged . . . must have been terrible and expressed a profound hatred since, one day, you decided to stop talking to one another and to use scribbled notes when it was necessary to communicate. When I speak of hatred, I do not exaggerate. . . . when a man and a woman who live together, united by marriage, reach the point at which each one prepares his own food, each one has his own larder which is locked with a key, and waits for the kitchen to be empty to eat, how can you explain that. . . . You were both afraid of being poisoned. It had become a morbid idée fixe.[19]

Simenon felt great resentment for his mother, whom he described as a very nervous woman, subject to brutal outbursts of anger. He felt that she was wrong to take in boarders and thereby deprive his father of a corner to call his own. Her temperament, her obsessions and ambitions, her tics and virtues are found in many of Simenon's fictional wives and mothers, but she is one of the few to be analyzed in depth. Women, in all of Simenon's other novels, with the exception of *La Vieille* and *Betty*, serve merely as catalysts, provoking the reactions of the males, since, for the author, it is the destiny of the male that is paramount.

In *Lettre à ma mère*, a poignant farewell written by Simenon to his mother three years after she died at the age of ninety-one, Simenon observes: "We never loved one another when you were alive, you know it well. Both of us only pretended."[20] *Lettre* transcribes the thoughts of the seventy-one year old author as he sits in her hospital room attempting to understand the woman who has always remained a stranger to him. He no longer judges her without pity: "I know now that there was never malice on your part, nor egotism. You were following your destiny."[21] His mother, like her father and like most of her brothers and sisters, was the victim of inherited neurotic traits. Instead of the vain defense of alcohol chosen by many of them, Henriette, the youngest, who had witnessed the struggle of the family and its progressive decay, decided that it was up to her alone to achieve her salvation. In a moving epitaph, Simenon pays final tribute to his mother: "You followed the course of your life with rare fidelity . . . you succeeded."[22]

V *Désiré Simenon*

While Simenon inherited from his mother her anxiety and her hypersensitivity, he is ashamed of her lack of dignity and of her hypocrisy. It is his father whom he adores and respects. Désiré Simenon, the thirteenth child of a Walloon family, is very different from Elise. He seemed "to be accompanied always by music which he alone heard and with which his regular steps kept time. Beneath his mustache, his avid lips half opened in a vague smile which expressed complete inner contentment."[23] From his father, Simenon inherited the contemplative side of his nature, his feeling of kinship with the world. Like Désiré, he is "sensitive to the quality of the air, to far off sounds, to moving spots of sunlight."[24]

Désiré is head clerk in a small insurance company. When he was asked by his employer to choose between fire and life insurance, he chose the former because life insurance was very new at the time. Life insurance becomes the more lucrative branch by far and Désiré's colleague, in a lesser position, earns much more than he. Elise continually reproaches Désiré for having chosen unwisely, reminding him that they have only "the bare necessities of life." But Désiré is happy, "happy in his household . . . happy in the street where he envies no one, happy in his office where he knows he is first."[25]

"My father went to his office exactly as he would have gone to heaven," Simenon writes. "He was the Just. . . . Despite the mediocrity of our life, he was at peace with himself and with others. My mother and a few of her sisters always wanted more."[26] In *Les Quatre jours du pauvre homme*, Simenon similarly describes Lecoin's father: "Through his glasses, he looked straight in front of him, with a look that was both strong and kind at the same time, with the shadow of a smile on his features. . . . People who smile like that, with that kind of sweetness, are people who have given up once and for all, given up fighting or expecting anything from anyone."[27]

Désiré lends his dignity, his quiet courage, his taste for a calm, regular, contemplative life, his family feeling to many of Simenon's protagonists, especially Maigret. "Until the very end, he kept his smiling serenity, he inhaled the joy of life wherever it presented itself as naturally as others breathe."[28]

VI   Two Clans

Simenon tells not only the story of his immediate family in *Pedigree*, but also that of two clans, the Walloon Mamelins (Simenons) and the Flemish Peters (Brülls), the twenty-four uncles and aunts, their spouses, and the sixty first cousins with whom he grew up. The Mamelins are pure Walloons, attached to their city and the working class Outremeuse district of Liége in which they live; they are "not people who move and who change occupations. They are suspicious of everything that moves. One is what one is, once and for all, employee, cabinetmaker, hatter, rich or poor."[29] They are a tightly knit clan under the domination of the mother and are very different from the Peters who, at Herstal, had been rich, having had as many as four barges on the canal to transport their logs and a stable filled with horses. One of the sons, Albert, went hunting with nobles, while another, Léopold, a strong-minded individual, was a waiter in Spa. The Peters are less united as a family; almost all are merchants, and self-interest and jealousy often set them against one another. These restless, anguished, maladjusted members of his mother's family, seeking to escape through drink, vagabondage, and power, serve as prototypes for Simenon's characters.

Elise's oldest brother, Léopold, who is thirty years older than she, remembers the years of wealth and tells her stories about their enormous home in Holland, an hour's walk from the closest dwelling. "The canal, which goes from Maestricht to Herzogenbosch, passes in front of the house, much higher than the land, and the boats you see gliding past reach to the tops of the poplars and always, particularly when the wind fills their sails, seem about to capsize into the fields."[30]

At that time, Léopold was a handsome young man who was studying at the university and socializing with the nobility. Suddenly, he decided to become a soldier, although the number he had drawn exempted him from service. For some inexplicable reason, he sold himself to replace another recruit, and subsequently married the canteen girl of his regiment. This terrible scandal provoked a rupture between Léopold and his family. In between stints as a waiter, he would disappear for six months or a year at a time and no one, including Eugénie, his wife, would hear from him. She would get a job, and when he returned he would put an ad in the newspaper to find her. She never reproached him and they would take up life together again until his wanderlust got the better of him and he would disappear once again.

One day, Léopold disappears forever; he dies of cancer of the tongue (a sickness that will reappear continually in Simenon's work, as will his Aunt Cécile's dropsy and his father's enlarged heart). A few weeks after his death, Eugénie's body is found in her room, where she has starved herself to death. "Eugénie, the canteen girl, had let herself die for love at the age of sixty, a few weeks after the final departure of Léopold, who had left so often before."[31] This love, which Simenon considers the greatest he ever encountered, was to inspire one of his few portrayals of true love and one of his best novels, *Le Grand Bob.*

Léopold is also at the origin of a very important theme in Simenon's work, the theme of flight. He is the prototype of those who have total scorn for all social life and all socially acceptable behavior. For Simenon, "there is something great about that strength of character to accept daily humiliation, or rather, not to feel that humiliation."[32] It is evident, he maintains, "that the true tramp is a more complete man than we. . . . He [Léopold] was a nonconformist. . . . The tramp is the man who lives without making any concessions, and who can live according to his own personal canons."[33]

Several of Simenon's aunts were also to inspire cycles of novels. "For a certain time, we would see a good deal of an aunt 'on my father's side' . . . then suddenly we wouldn't see her any longer and we would spend every Sunday at the home of a different aunt 'on my mother's side'. . . . There was the Aunt Françoise period, the Aunt Marthe period, the Aunt Madeleine period, and the Aunt Anna period."[34] Aunt Marie (Aunt Louisa in *Pedigree)* had a grocery store/bar on the Coronmeuse quai where she would supply the boatmen whose boats were moored above the locks. The memory of that neighborhood has remained stronger and more vivid for Simenon than that of the neighborhood in which he grew up:

The Coronmeuse quai, and with it the canal, the port where one or two hundred canal boats, perhaps even more, stand side by side, at times ten deep, with laundry drying, children playing, dogs napping, an invigorating odor of tar and resin. . . . There is the old-fashioned store window, cluttered with merchandise, starch, candles, packages of chicory, bottles of vinegar. There is the glazed door and its transparent advertisement: the white lion of Rémy starch, the zebra of an oven cleaner, the other lion, the black one, of a brand of wax. . . . Above all, the unique, the marvelous odor of this house where nothing is unimportant, where everything is exceptional, where everything is rare. . . . Is it the smell of gin that predominates? Is it of the more insipid groceries? For they sell everything, there is everything in the store, barrels of American oil, rope, stable lanterns, whips, and tar for boats. There are jars of candy of an uncertain pink color and glass drawers stuffed with cinnamon sticks and cloves.[35]

Mixed with these odors is the smell of willows, since Uncle Lunel is a basketmaker. Lunel, like Léopold, has fled, but he has done so while remaining behind, taking refuge from the world in his deafness. In *Chez Krull, Chez les Flamands*, and many other novels, including several Maigrets, Simenon will evoke this combination grocery store/bar, women like Aunt Louisa, and men like Uncle Lunel.

Another sister, Aunt Marthe, the one for whom Elise worked when she was young, is the wife of a wealthy wholesale grocer, Hubert Schroefs. They live in a "huge house of white brick, just opposite the meat market, with the wholesale grocery store and the main entrance from which the trucks come out. And on the canvas covering of these trucks there is the name of my uncle in enormous letters."[36] Aunt Marthe will provide inspiration for a long line of alcoholic women who periodically go on binges, referred to as "novenas" in the family's lexicon, while Schroefs's lineage will include the wealthy, arrogant, cruel individuals found in *Le Riche homme, Le Bourgemestre de Furnes*, and *Oncle Charles s'est enfermé*.

Marthe is not the only one of Elise's sisters who drinks. Félicie, the prettiest and the one closest in age to Elise, is also an alcoholic. "Poor Félicie, in truth the most unfortunate, also the prettiest, the most moving of my aunts, whom I still see leaning her elbows on the counter of her beautiful café in a pose filled with romantic nostalgia."[37] Félicie is married to the owner of a bar who torments and beats her and finally drives her mad. Roger is present when they take her in a straight jacket to the hospital—where she will die of delirium tremens—while her husband is led off to jail. The protagonists of *Malempin* and *Faubourg* will witness similar scenes:

There were many people in the house, aunts and uncles, also people he didn't know. They were speaking softly, mysteriously. You would have said that a crime had been committed. Then they heard a piercing female shriek, a cry of terror, and he saw his aunt . . . carried down the stairs by two male nurses. . . . During this time, his uncle, the one he had never seen before . . . sobbed, leaning against the wall, all alone in a shadowy corner of the corridor.

For a year, when they passed in front of the house, his mother repeated to him:

—He was your uncle. . . . But you must never speak of him. . . . Because of him, your aunt went mad.[38]

Alcoholism, this insatiable form of self-destruction, this effort made by many of his maternal aunts and uncles to flee from themselves, is one of Simenon's principal themes. In *Quand j'étais vieux*, a journal that Simenon kept for the years 1960 - 62,[39] he wrote that of all the dangers he ran in the course of his life, alcoholism was undoubtedly the most serious. "I have studied the question as only specialists have done, in the domain of criminology also. . . . Perhaps because I just missed becoming an alcoholic,"[40] he added. Simenon never drank until he became a reporter and drank only moderately until he began the first Maigrets, at which time he developed the habit of drinking wine. "I was rarely drunk, but I needed a pick-me-up as early as the morning, especially to write."[41] However, it was not until he came to America that he became an alcoholic:

I'm speaking of a particular, almost permanent state, in which one is dominated by alcohol, whether during the hours one is drinking, or during the hours when one is impatiently waiting to drink, almost as painfully as the drug addict waits for his injection or his fix. . . . If one has never known this experience, it is difficult to understand American life. The crowds cease to be anonymous, the bars cease to be ordinary, ill-lit places, the taxi drivers complaining or menacing people. From one end of the country to the other there exists a freemasonry of alcoholics. . . . It's another world in which certain preoccupations disappear, where the importance of things changes.[42]

Simenon deals with "this other world," both in the United States and France, in *Feux rouges*, *Antoine et Julie*, *Le Fond de la bouteille*, *Betty*, *Le Déménagement*, and others.

VII   *Elise's Boarders*

Elise's boarders as well as the members of the Mamelin and Peters clans were to serve as models for many of Simenon's fictional

characters. These young men and women came from Eastern
Europe to study in Liége because it was the least expensive of the
French-speaking university cities. Some of them were also there to
pursue their revolutionary activities. Frida Stavitskaïa, Elise's first
boarder, belonged to a group of nihilists, and her father was a
political prisoner in Siberia. The same Frida would become a doctor
and a People's Commissar in Communist Russia, which would have
amazed Elise, who noticed only her bad manners and her peculiar
diet of eggs and tap water. There were also Schascher, a timid red-
headed Russian Jew; Saft, a blond Pole; Bogdanowski, obese and in-
solent, of uncertain nationality; Lola, remote and sensual; Mlle
Feinstein, vulgar, narcissistic, and a gifted mathematician. These
foreign students or their counterparts appear in *Le Locataire, La
Nuit du carrefour, Crime impuni, Les Fiançailles de M. Hire, Le
Petit Homme d'Arkhangelsk, Les Inconnus dans la maison, Maigret
et son mort,* and *Pietr-le-Letton.*

Pietr, the Lett, is described as a typical Northern type. Commissaire Maigret had studied several of that sort, all of them in-
tellectuals, and those with whom he had associated during his brief
career as a medical student had baffled his Latin nature.

He remembered one of them, among others, a thin, blond Pole whose hair
was already sparse at the age of twenty-two, whose mother was a
charwoman in his country, and who, for seven whole years, took courses at
the Sorbonne, without socks on his feet, eating nothing but a piece of bread
and an egg each day.

He could not buy the written courses and he had to study in the public
libraries.

He knew nothing of Paris, neither the women nor the French character.
But he had hardly finished his studies when he was offered an important
professorship in Warsaw. Five years later, Maigret saw him return to Paris,
as dry and as cold, in a delegation of foreign scientists and he dined at the
Elysée Palace.

The Commissaire had known others. All were not of equal worth, but
almost all astonished him by the number and diversity of things that they
wanted to learn and that they learned.

To study . . . for the sake of studying. . . . There was that kind of will
in the grey-green eves of the Lett.[43]

Many of his mother's boarders were medical students and they
introduced Simenon to the study of medicine and psychology. The
medical books he read at that time, including Testut's *Treatise on*

Anatomy, gave him the biological knowledge of man that is one of the keys to his work. When asked by an interviewer whether he could have been anything other than a novelist, Simenon replied:

I could have been a doctor, a diagnostician, not a specialist. I would have liked to diagnose illnesses and I must confess that I have had occasion to do so.

When I am in someone's presence I wonder: "What's wrong with him?" and I look for pathological causes.

What delighted me most of all that has been written or said about me was a remark by Professor Leriche: "What pleases me in your books, Simenon, is the fact that your characters have not only a romantic, intellectual, or animal life, but a liver, lungs, a heart, muscles, nerves. I try to diagnose them at the first chapter, curious to know at the end whether or not I was wrong."[44]

Simenon feels that the doctor and the novelist are similar in that they are the only ones to examine men closely.

VIII   *Roger Mamelin (Simenon)*

While the first two-thirds of *Pedigree* are dominated by the figure of Elise, the third part presents a highly detailed portrait of Roger. "When I wrote *Pedigree*," Simenon observed, "I had a second reason for doing so . . . when it was finished, I said to myself: 'I've finally finished with all those people. Now that I have put them into a book in the flesh, they no longer encumber me and I am going to be able to write about new and different characters'. . . . [However] I never completely got rid of Roger in *Pedigree* for we are one to a certain extent. Other than in *Pedigree*, I never put myself into my novels."[45]

Roger had always been ashamed of his mother, of the way she cheated her boarders, of her constant whining and complaining, of her calculating treatment of others depending upon their social status, of her lack of pride, and of her hypocrisy. Coupled with shame is the feeling of impotence experienced by the small boy before the domineering woman, and the desire to free himself. His mother's emasculating nature will leave an indelible imprint on him and affect his judgment of all women, whom he will regard as adversaries. Consciously or unconsciously, they try to enter into man's inner, private life. While Roger's humiliation takes the form of an inferiority complex, he begins to adopt an increasingly aggressive attitude toward his mother. Not infrequently, he will berate her, shouting: "Yes, you are a beggar. It's in your blood. Even when you don't need anything, you look as if you're asking for something. You have to talk about the bare necessities, preferably to Aunt Louisa because you know that anything that humiliates father pleases her. . . . You're going to remind me of your prolapsus of the womb again, aren't you? Is it my fault if you have trouble with your organs, as you put it so delicately?"[46]

Roger's rebellion against his mother occurs at the same time as his sexual awakening and causes a psychic crisis that will have a profound effect on the portrayal of women and sexuality in Simenon's work. Parinaud has analyzed this crisis as follows: "Woman is both the enemy and the desired object. In order to be possessed, she must also be humiliated to be brought down to the level of the male. Therefore, he wants a woman who has been soiled."[47] This is why there are so many men in Simenon's work who are impotent other than with whores, many who even marry whores, and others who become infatuated with fallen women. Sexuality in Simenon's work is always described with the pitiless crudity of this adolescent vision.

There is also a certain masochistic side to Roger's rebellion against his mother. He is obsessed by a desire to sink further and further into vice. His despair leads to an attempt at moral suicide—he steals, he sells black market merchandise, he frequents German soldiers and whores and delights defiantly in his shame. Yet, even during his worst moments of debauchery, Roger feels a nostalgia for something better. "It seemed to him that all that was needed was an effort made once and for all, and then there would be no rotters any more, life would be beautiful and clean, as harmonious as certain memories, and you would no longer have the impression of constantly floundering about in filth."[48] He wonders at times what he can do to make life beautiful and clean, above all clean. He feels that his life is somewhere else, he doesn't know where, but he decides that he will keep on looking for it.[49] While the rebellious Roger is the prototype of the adolescents in Simenon's work who feel the need to escape from the pettiness and meanness of their milieu and to lead violent lives, the Roger who longs for purity and order will be the inspiration for Alain Malou (*Le Destin des Malou*).

It is Roger's father who finally saves him. One morning he returns home after a night of debauchery and learns that his father has had a heart attack. As he enters Désiré's room, it seems to Roger that his father is silently transmitting the message: " 'You see, son, I have saved you.' For Roger is saved, at present, he is sure of it."[50] In effect, Désiré has become the sacrificial victim who will redeem Roger. "From one minute to the next, everything that a little while ago seemed so fraught with potential tragedy works out. . . . He will no longer go to school. He will not have to take his exams, nor suffer the disgrace of an inevitable failure."[51] The theme of paternal salvation presented in *Pedigree* is found in many of Simenon's novels, among them *L'Âne Rouge, Le Fils, La Neige était sale*, and is implicit in all of the Maigrets. Désiré, the father, the comrade, forgives all trespasses and has the ability to exorcize the evil possessing the son. Roger draws back from the edge of the precipice; he will enter the world and seek a place in society. "I am going to be a man, I promise you,"[52] he tells his father. The leitmotif of Simenon's work, "It is a difficult job to be a man,"[53] attests to the difficulty of this endeavor.

In an interview with Brendan Gill, Simenon said: "I was born in the dark and the rain, and I got away. The crimes I write about—sometimes I think they are the crimes I would have committed if I had not got away. I am one of the lucky ones. What is there to say about the lucky ones except that they got away?"[54] It is Simenon's awareness of the thin line separating the criminal from "those who got away" that governs his refusal to pass judgment. He wants his readers to understand that they, too, could be driven to the limit and, as a result, to ask themselves the question: "Why he and not I?"

Pedigree ends with the armistice of 1918. Roger is sixteen years old. His father's health makes it essential for him to leave school and find a job. The details of his remaining years in Liége may be found in the novels *Les Trois crimes de mes amis, Le Pendu de Saint-Pholien*, and *L'Âne rouge*. In the first two, Simenon tells the story of the clique of young poets and painters calling themselves "The Keg," who met in a room in a ruined house behind the Saint-Pholien Church. Every one of Simenon's friends in "The Keg" was to fail in life. At seventy-two, looking back on his life, Simenon wrote that this was one of the reasons why failure became an obsession with him. "I knew too many of them in my adolescence, then later on during my early years in Paris, then even later on, and even today. I was afraid of becoming one of them for years. . . . The failure, for me, is the man who had great ambitions in one field or another, who was enthusiastic, who sacrificed everything, and who, one day, years later, realizes that he hasn't arrived anywhere."[55]

While the members of "The Keg" were all to be failures, three other men whom Simenon knew were to become murderers. In *Les Trois crimes de mes amis*, Simenon tells the story of these men and wonders whether the time in which they lived can serve as explanation for their crimes. "Are there periods of more intense ferment, or moments when unhealthy currents flow? . . . I am inclined to believe it, above all since, in the youth I knew, I find in all of my friends, only less accentuated, the very thing that made criminals of those I mentioned. What gave us that taste for fallen women, the most disgusting love affairs . . . that unhealthy exaltation between two glasses of wine? . . . Wasn't it the fault of the war that we lived through as children without understanding it and that marked us without our realizing it?"[56]

Simenon worked for a brief period for a newspaper, *La Cravache (The Horsewhip)*, but left it in 1919, when he discovered that it was a blackmail sheet, to join the staff of the respectable *Gazette de Liége*. He graduated rapidly from cub reporter to his own column, "Hors du poulailler" ("From the Hen Roost"), which he signed M. le Coq. In 1922, he went to Paris. "I realized that only what one has lived oneself can be transmitted to others through literature. I had to know the world from every angle, horizontally and vertically . . . know it in all its dimensions, come into contact with countries and races, climates and customs, but also to penetrate it vertically . . . have access to different social strata, to be as much at ease in a tiny fisherman's bistro as at an agricultural fair or in a banker's living room."[57]

In the early twenties, Simenon began submitting stories to the newspaper *Le Matin*, edited at that time by Colette. She told him that his stories were too pretentious, that he should avoid striving for literary effect and make his work simple by paring it down to what was absolutely essential. When he followed her advice, which he feels was the most useful he received in his life, Simenon's stories were accepted for publication. Also during these years, Simenon began to write pulp fiction. The series of popular novels he wrote between 1925 and 1934 under a series of pseudonyms were, for Simenon, an apprenticeship in his craft. Instead of working at another job that would permit him to write, as many artists and writers do, he was working in his own field.

Until the outbreak of the Second World War, Simenon traveled continually. He followed the canals of France from north to south and from east to west, and traveled throughout the rest of Europe, Africa, Panama, the United States, Tahiti, New Zealand, Australia, India, Russia, Turkey, and Egypt. All of these countries would provide settings for his novels. However, Simenon maintains that he was not traveling in search of the picturesque and that only very few of his novels are exotic. Among these he includes *Les Clients d'Avrenos* (Turkey), *Quartier Nègre* (Panama), *Le Coup de lune* (Gabon), *45°à l'ombre* (sea route from Matadi to Bordeaux), *L'Aîné des Ferchaux* (Congo, Panama), *Ceux de la soif* (the Galapagos), *Touriste de bananes* (Tahiti), *Long Cours* (Panama and Tahiti), *Le Passager clandestin* (Tahiti). Even in these, however, the exotic element does not play a great part. "I maintain that when one lives in a place, a tree is a tree, whether it is called a kapok tree, a flame tree, or an oak. Local color exists only for people who are passing through. And I hate being a tourist. I am not seeking the sense of being abroad. On the contrary, I am looking for what is similar in man, the constant."[58] In several series of articles inspired by his travels, Simenon rid himself of what he didn't want to put into his novels, the picturesque and "some more or less philosophical or political cogitations."[59]

Simenon came to the United States in 1945, where he met Denise Ouimet, a French Canadian who became his second wife and mother of three of his four children. His novel *Trois Chambres à Manhattan,* written the following year, is a love story with a happy ending and is one of the author's favorite works. Their travels throughout the United States provided the background for a series of novels set in various regions of the United States: *La Jument perdue, Le Fond de la bouteille, Maigret chez le coroner, Un Nouveau dans la ville, La Mort de Belle, L'Horloger d'Everton, La Boule noire, La Main, Maigret à New York, Trois Chambres à Manhattan, Feux rouges, Les Frères Rico,* and *Crime impuni* (second half).

Simenon and his family returned to Europe in 1957 and settled on a large property near Lausanne. Drawn by an irresistible desire to go back to his origins, Simenon sold his estate in 1972, a few years after Denise's nervous breakdown, and bought a small eighteenth century house with small rooms and a mansard roof. "I was born and raised in a small, modest house. I am returning to my roots and that delights me."[60] He lives there with his youngest son and his companion of the last ten years, Theresa, with whom he feels that he has found the love he was seeking throughout his life.

"For me, an old man who has had the time to think and reflect,"
Simenon writes, "love is silence first of all. It is the ability to stay
together in the same room without speaking, each one conscious of
the other's thoughts . . . it is a hand that unconsciously seeks the
other's body in sleep, not for sexual reasons, but only for contact. . . . [It is] complete spiritual and physical contact. It is thinking of the same things together, experiencing the same reactions,
the same emotions, and seeking the reflection of these emotions in
the other's eyes."[61]

In 1973, Simenon announced that he would no longer write
novels because of his recurring bouts with Ménière's disease and
also because he felt that after fifty years he had become a slave of
his characters. "All of my life, I was preoccupied with others and
tried to understand them. Now, I am trying to understand
myself."[62] His last five works, *Lettre à ma mère, Des traces de pas,
Un Homme comme un autre, Les Petits hommes, Vent du nord-
Vent du sud,* are made up of observations and reflections on his own
life. By means of these works, he is trying, as so many others have
done, to acquire insight into the literary phenomenon named
Georges Simenon.

CHAPTER 2

Maigret—Mender
of Destinies

I   *Creation of Maigret*

S IMENON wrote the early Maigret novels as a bridge between the popular potboilers he had been writing and the more
serious literary efforts to which he aspired and for which he did not
consider himself ready. They were, in a sense, an apprenticeship for
more ambitious works to come. Not knowing at that time how to
shift the action from one location to another, he had the idea of
creating a character who could move about freely without requiring
justification to do so and decided that a policeman would answer
the purpose very well. He proposed the Maigrets to Fayard
publishers and, in 1929, signed a contract with them for eighteen
novels. The following year, he launched the series with a party, an
"anthropometric ball,"[1] to which he invited all the Parisian
celebrities.

While Simenon originally intended to abandon the genre after
fulfilling his contract, he returned to his policeman hero in sixty-five
more novels and eighteen short stories, often trying out in them
themes and situations he would use later on in his more serious
works. Before considering the "Maigrets," a word that has passed
into current usage to designate Simenon's detective novels, it is
necessary to describe the genre in order to demonstrate the way in
which Simenon transformed its rules and techniques and used it to
express the most important themes of the twentieth century
novel—guilt and innocence, alienation and solitude.

II   *A Brief History of the Detective Novel*

While the detective novel has been defined in many different
ways, all definitions agree that, basically, it is a fictitious prose

narrative of an investigation that reveals to the reader how and by whom the crime was committed. Although Poe's *The Murders in the Rue Morgue* is considered by many the first of the genre, it was actually preceded by Balzac's *Histoire des treize*, which is perhaps the archetype. Thus, the birth of the detective novel, which postulates the existence of a hidden truth to be uncovered, occurred during the height of Romanticism with its glorification of the forces of darkness and mystery and its fascinating mythology of the criminal. Romanticism exalted the superman, whether bandit or policeman, both of whom were outside the normal order of society,[2] and both of whom possessed the extraordinary perspicacity and energy that would characterize detective literature, a literature still dominated by the figure of the superior man.

In the post-Romantic period, detective novels changed radically, giving the powers of reason precedence over the powers of darkness. It was Poe who created the detective novel that glorified the intellect and showed that all mysteries can be solved by pure intelligence. He established the format of a type of detective novel that is still popular. It would begin with a seemingly insoluble mystery; then, a series of witnesses and suspects would appear who would throw out false clues; finally, the detective, by careful reasoning, would arrive at the correct, irrefutable, enlightening, and completely unexpected conclusion.

The next great writer of mystery novels was Arthur Conan Doyle, whose novels are contemporary with the first major advances of modern science. Science brought with it the promise that man would eventually solve all of his problems by applying to them the scientific method. Sherlock Holmes, with his microscopic vision and his impeccable reasoning powers, has been called the scientific detective. His success is based on unerring observation, complete concentration, and encyclopedic knowledge. Holmes's brain resembles a gigantic computer into which all human knowledge has been fed and which can automatically solve all problems by relating cause and effect.

The detective novel was to change again in the wake of the disillusionment with science that followed World War I. At the same time, faith in reason was diminishing as Freud gave primacy to the irrational forces of the unconscious. New methods of investigation that relied on instinct, intuition, and empathy replaced rational deduction. Simenon's Maigret, who has been called the Bergson of the detective novel,[3] illustrates this change in emphasis. Maigret's role, unlike that of Holmes, is not to reason but to understand intuitively.[4]

III   *The Mender of Destinies*

Maigret's infinite understanding and compassion can be traced to a need Simenon felt in his youth:

When I was fourteen . . . I wondered why there did not exist a type of doctor who would be both a doctor of the body and of the mind, a sort of doctor who, knowing an individual, his age, his physical characteristics, his potentialities, could tell him to enter on one course or another.

It was virtually psychosomatic medicine that I was formulating. That was in 1917, and it was in that frame of mind that I created the character of Maigret. For that is what Maigret does, and this is why it was necessary for Maigret to have completed two or three years of medical studies. . . . Maigret is for me a mender of destinies.[5]

Maigret's ability "to live the lives of every sort of man, to put himself inside everybody's mind"[6] remains constant throughout the Maigret cycle, as do Maigret's methods. While the technique remains essentially the same, there is a change in emphasis from the early novels, where Maigret is solely a sympathetic witness, to the later works in which he occupies the entire novel and his reactions, rather than the case at hand, hold the reader's attention. Maigret becomes the novelist Simenon, in a sense, and comports himself accordingly. Like Simenon, he seeks to find the man hidden beneath surface appearances; like Simenon, he writes down the principal elements of a case on an envelope; like Simenon, he finds that as a case proceeds he begins to resemble the characters. Brigid Brophy has stated that Simenon made Maigret a detective rather than a novelist because the detective is the only one who can actually approach the murder victim. Maigret has the novelist's passivity—while other detectives sit and think, he sits and imagines.[7] When Maigret follows a suspect, he is not waiting for him to commit the blunder that will facilitate his apprehension, but is attempting to feel with the suspect, to adapt to the rhythm of his life, and to understand him. Unlike other detectives, he does not try to set up barriers between the criminal and himself, but, on the contrary, seeks to remove them.

IV   Le Charretier de "la Providence"

One of the earliest Maigrets, *Le Charretier de "la Providence,"* provides an excellent introduction to the methods, or nonmethods, of Maigret. It reveals that the essence of an investigation of a crime for Maigret is not who did it or how he did it, but why he did it.

The rain has been falling steadily for two days when Maigret begins his investigation at lock number 14, connecting the Marne and the lateral canal. The body of an elegantly dressed woman without identification papers has been found in a stable for cart horses, which can be reached only by a narrow path. Since his arrival on the scene, Maigret has been familiarizing himself with a world that is completely new to him, that of canals and inland water transportation. In a manner that characterizes the first stage of all of his investigations, Maigret sits in the local café soaking up the atmosphere, inhaling "a distinctive odor, the nature of which was enough to mark the difference between this and a country café. It smelled of stables, harnesses, tar and groceries, oil and gas."[8] As he sits in the café, he watches the barges continue peacefully on their way from lock to lock pulled by horses. Maigret's ruminations are interrupted by the arrival in the café of the owner of a yacht, Sir William Lampson, who identifies the dead woman as his wife who had left the yacht a few days before.

The next day, Maigret is joined at the lock by Inspector Lucas, who will become a familiar figure in the Maigret entourage. He informs the commissaire that the Englishman lives only for whisky and women and that his companion, Willy Marco, is a well-known swindler. When Willy is also found strangled, the second stage of Maigret's inquiry begins: certain events become clearer, a few of the characters come to the forefront, and the reader is led to believe that he is independently reaching the same conclusions as Maigret. Following his intuition, Maigret questions Jean, the carter of the barge "Providence," and accuses him of having killed Marco. Jean throws himself into the lock basin. He is rescued, but flees from the hospital to which he has been taken in order to die in the stable of the "Providence." Maigret, in the meantime, takes his fingerprints and discovers that he was formerly a physician who had spent time in jail.

Maigret returns to the stable and tells the dying carter to confirm his statements by blinking his eyelids. Then, Maigret begins a long monologue as he reconstructs the events leading up to the murder of Mary Lampson. Jean, after many years, saw his wife, who had promised to wait for him when he went to jail, living with Colonel Lampson under the name of Mary Lampson. The carter, who had almost forgotten his previous identity, felt the need to bring down to his level the woman who had betrayed him. He brought Mary Lampson back to the stable where she stayed for three days, afraid of Jean and ashamed of her past actions. Finally, unable to stand such a life any longer, she rebelled and he killed her rather than permit her to leave him again. In order to divert suspicion from himself, Jean stole a sailor's hat which he planted in the stable. He was forced to kill Willy because he had witnessed the theft. Then, as Jean felt Maigret closing in on him, he attempted suicide.

Maigret explains to Colonel Lampson why Jean fled the hospital. "A man without ties . . . a man who cut all links with his past, with his former personality . . . must hang on to something. . . . He had his stable . . . the smell . . . the horses . . . the burning hot coffee swallowed at three in the morning before walking until evening. . . . His burrow as it were . . . filled with his animal warmth. . . . There are burrows of all sorts. . . . There are those that smell of whisky, eau de cologne, and women. . . ."[9] As he explains, Maigret feels the same sympathy for this worthless, alcoholic aristocrat as he does for Jean, for Lampson is as much alone, as much at a loss as Jean. This ability to understand is Maigret's outstanding virtue. His sympathy extends to all but the very few gratuitously wicked individuals he meets.

V *Gratuitous Evil*

In *Maigret se défend*, his friend, Dr. Pardon, asks Maigret whether he ever encountered a "pure" criminal, one who was entirely responsible for his actions and was evil for the sake of evil. When Maigret asks whether he means a pure criminal according to the criminal code, Pardon answers: "No, according to you."[10] Maigret remarks hesitantly that if he been obliged to become a magistrate or a member of a jury, he is certain he could not take it upon himself to judge another person, no matter what the crime, since it is not the crime that counts but what is taking place, or what has taken place within the person who committed the crime. Furthermore, he adds that what seems to be evil at first sight becomes understandable as the facts become known. The remainder of the novel serves to prove this thesis.

On returning home, Maigret finds a summons to appear before the préfet de police, who launches into an attack on Maigret's unorthodox, out-of-date methods. His real purpose, however, is to ask Maigret to resign because of a complaint he received from a high government official whose niece signed a complaint against Maigret for sexual abuse. At first glance, this seems to be the case of pure wickedness postulated in Pardon's theoretical question, for this could be the only explanation for the desire of an obviously sane girl to harm Maigret. The reason for her actions slowly comes to light, reaffirming Simenon's thesis that crime is not so much willful sin as the product of sickness or unbearable pressure.

Maigret discovers that the girl had been driven to this action by blackmail. Her abortionist had seen Maigret across the street from his office where Maigret had been staking out a gang of jewel thieves. Because he feared that Maigret was watching him and would discover not only the nature of his practice but also the bodies of several victims buried in his garden, he had devised the bizarre plot to discredit Maigret. Here, as in all of his cases, Maigret's investigation centers not on events but on an exploration of personality, since his interest lies more in understanding the criminal than in solving the crime. His inquiry reinforces his belief that he who murders is an unfortunate being, for "every man is capable of becoming a murderer if he has sufficient motivation."[11]

VI   *The Victim*

The psychological makeup of the victim interests Maigret as much as that of the criminal. "I will know the murderer when I know the victim well,"[12] he once said. In *Maigret et l'homme tout seul*, the dead man is the center of interest and the solution of the crime comes almost as an afterthought. The victim is a derelict, murdered in a filthy, condemned house in one of the oldest sections of Paris. The corpse, however, is immaculately clean. Maigret surmises that the motive for the killing must lie in a remote past when something so shattering happened that it turned a healthy man into a tramp.

When the tramp's picture is circulated, Maigret discovers that he was a certain Marcel Vivien, a cabinetmaker, who disappeared at the end of 1945. Maigret interviews the man's wife, daughter, and neighbors and reads newspapers of the period, attempting to form a picture in his mind of Vivien's character. Maigret learns that Vivien had left his wife and child destitute to go off with another woman. Soon afterward, a young painter also became her lover, and Vivien, who had forsaken his family for her, begged her to leave the other man. When she refused, he killed her. Years later, the painter, who had never forgotten the girl, saw Vivien loading vegetables at Les Halles and shot him. Here, as in all of the Maigrets, the criminal kills because he cannot do otherwise.

Maigret's sympathy extends to both the victim and the murderer, for he understands the passion that drove two ordinary men to kill. Vivien's responsibility for his death is also apparent, bearing out Simenon's contention, and that of many criminologists, that "there are at least eight crimes in ten in which the victim shares to a great extent the responsibility of the murderer."[13] Simenon writes that one of the branches of criminology least known to the general public is victimology, that is to say, the responsibility of the victim in crimes.[14] Often, as in *Maigret in Vichy*, the victim, who had goaded her murderer beyond endurance, is more villainous than the murderer. At the end of the novel, Maigret expresses the hope that the murderer will be acquitted.

Maigret is similarly disinclined to bring to justice Fumal's murderer in *Un échec de Maigret*. "What troubled Maigret most was the wickedness he felt behind all of Fumal's doings, for he had always resisted believing in pure evil."[15] He is, of course, curious to know which of the many people who had sufficient motivation had finally decided to do away with Fumal, but he knows that he will feel pangs of conscience when he is obliged to arrest the murderer.

The murdered wine merchant in *Maigret et le marchand de vin* is also a person whose psychological compulsions to use his power and money to humiliate those dependent on him would identify him as a natural victim. The merchant had surrounded himself only with people whom he could despise. Every sexual encounter represented an attempt to defile his partner and to assert his dominance. When his secretary had asked him why he went out of his way to make people hate him, he answered that he did so because he could not make them love him, and that he preferred hatred to indifference.[16]

The murderer seeks to approach Maigret, circling closer and closer. At the same time, Maigret begins to understand, or rather to feel intuitively, the psychological background of the crime. His choice of clues is revealing in this respect for he never looks for fingerprints, traces of blood, or footprints. Nor does he attempt to interrogate witnesses to pinpoint the exact moment the crime occurred. For Maigret, a clue is a gesture, a word spoken inadvertently, a look that he intercepts. His clues are a gradually developing awareness of the pressures exerted by a particular atmosphere that drive an ordinary human being to murder. Solving a crime for Maigret does not involve discovering the criminal's method, but attempting to relive the psychological crisis that provoked the crime. Putting himself in the criminal's place, Maigret asks himself whether he would make a certain gesture or say a certain word if he had committed the crime.[17] Simenon presents the precise psychological detail that makes the murderer an understandable, unforgettable human being. To underline that the traditional hunt of the "whodunit" is unimportant for Simenon, he frequently reveals the identity of the murderer at the beginning of the novel, devoting the remaining pages to the psychological analysis of the criminal that will convince the reader of the inevitability of his crime. As he discovers the truth, in such novels, the reader pities the murderer.

The murderer of the wine merchant had been an underdog all his life, never knowing what it meant to hold his head high. His desperate act, as is so often the case in Simenon's work, is the last resort of an ego threatened with disintegration. Having committed a murder, he has become important for the first time in his life. Maigret understands that men of his sort are terribly sensitive. "They long to talk, to make themselves understood, and yet, they don't really believe that there is anybody capable of understanding them."[18] When Maigret and the murderer finally come face to face, the latter reveals that he killed his employer because he had robbed him of his self-respect. He had degraded him to the point where he was ashamed to be alive. This theme of humiliation leading to murder is found in Simenon's serious novels, taking up in a major key, as is often the case in his work, themes treated in a minor key in the Maigrets.

VII   Maigret tend un piège

Simenon again focuses on human motivation in *Maigret tend un piège* as he adds a detective story plot to a novel of psychological analysis. While the police or detective hunt for a criminal in the traditional detective novel, Maigret looks for the man behind the criminal. He waits for the "human fissure" when the criminal cracks and the man who committed the crime is revealed in all his strength and weakness.[19]

The problem facing Maigret in this novel is a formidable one. In recent weeks, there have been five murders in a very small area of the eighteenth arrondissement of Paris. The pattern followed in each of the attacks has been identical: the victims, all women, have been stabbed to death, their clothing slashed to pieces. The only thing they have in common is their short, stocky build and the district in which they were murdered. Maigret asks a distinguished psychiatrist, Dr. Tissot, why the murderer suddenly changed on February second, the day of the first murder, from a harmless citizen into a dangerous maniac. Tissot replies that among all the murderers with whom he is familiar, there is one constant, a need to assert themselves, because almost all of them have been considered inferior in their own circle. Tissot adds that this common characteristic convinced him that the majority of crimes that seem to have no motive, particularly repeated crimes, are a manifestation of wounded pride. What he and his colleagues still do not understand is the process by which such long-suppressed humiliation suddenly erupts into crime. They believe, however, that such criminals are driven by a need to be caught because they cannot bear to think that those around them still think of them as ordinary, harmless individuals. Therefore, if someone were to take credit for the crime and be arrested in his place, the criminal would feel frustration at losing his claim to distinction.

Dr. Tissot's counsel leads Maigret to risk another murder, as he pretends to have arrested the criminal and then sets up one of his policewomen as a decoy in the murder area. Maigret counts on Tissot's assurance that maniacs, like most criminals, nearly always use the same technique, down to the smallest detail. The murderer does indeed attack the policewoman, who grabs a button from his jacket before he runs off. Without difficulty, Maigret is able to track down and arrest the murderer, an interior decorator named Moncin, who is identified positively by the policewoman. The identification of the criminal so early in the book is contrary to all of the rules of the detective novel, but, as in all of the Maigrets, it is not the identity of the criminal that is important, but the reasons for his crime.

The night of Moncin's arrest, another crime is committed, but with some variations. Presuming that either Moncin's mother or wife committed this murder to save him, Maigret reconstructs Moncin's psychological crisis. Performing the role of a psychiatrist, he tells the young man that his mother had been ashamed of his father, a butcher, and had brought him up as if he were a prince. She was there to protect and take care of him in any eventuality, but he had to pay for this with submissiveness. He was her property and he was not permitted to grow up to be a normal man. She married him off when he was twenty-four to a woman she thought she could control but who turned out to be as domineering and as possessive as she. "You hadn't the courage to be a man. You weren't one," Maigret remarks. "You needed them, the atmosphere they created around you, their attention, their indulgence. And that was precisely what humiliated you. When, why, under the stress of what emotion, of what humiliation worse than the others was the thing triggered? . . . Anyhow, a plan for asserting yourself came into your mind."[20] Maigret notes that Moncin couldn't assert himself in his career in which he was a failure. He could not kill his wife or mother because he would be the prime suspect. Since the action had to be something outstanding to satisfy his vanity, he turned to women in the street, using the knife because he needed "some furious, violent gesture."[21] He needed to destroy and to feel that he was destroying. He didn't rape his victims because he was impotent, but tore their undergarments to shreds. Ironically, his crimes did not free him from the domination of his wife and mother, one of whom had killed the sixth victim to protect her property. While both were capable of this action, it was the wife who acted, winning thereby the final round in her match with her mother-in-law.

VIII   *Absence of Professional Criminals*

There are very few members of the criminal class in Simenon's work, since his interest lies not in the professional but in the ordinary human being who is driven to crime. In *Les Mémoires de Maigret*, the commissaire reflects that the young Simenon told him he wasn't interested in professional criminals. "Their psychology doesn't present any problem. They are people who are doing their job, and that's that."[22] There is even a certain bond between the policeman and the professional criminal. Except in very rare cases, the policeman is entirely devoid of hatred or even of ill will. But, he is also devoid of pity in this strictly professional relationship. Paradoxically, a sort of family feeling often springs up between the policeman and his quarry:

The prostitute of the Boulevard de Clichy and the inspector watching her are both wearing cheap shoes and both have sore feet from the kilometers of pavement they've covered. They both put up with the same rain, the same icy wind. . . . It is the same with the pickpocket who slips through the crowd at the fairgrounds. For him, a fair or any gathering of a few hundred people represents not pleasure . . . but a certain number of wallets in unsuspecting pockets. The same is true for the policeman. And both of them recognize equally well at first glance the self-satisfied hick who will make an ideal victim.[23]

In some cases, a certain closeness is established between the policeman and his prisoner, stemming perhaps from the fact that for weeks, sometimes months, the policeman and the culprit have been almost exclusively preoccupied with one another. "The officer works unceasingly to delve more deeply into the past life of the guilty party, tries to reconstruct his thoughts, to anticipate his slightest reflexes. Both of them are playing for very high stakes. And when they meet, it is in circumstances dramatic enough to dissolve the polite indifference that presides over human relationships in everyday life."[24]

In a newspaper article of April 2, 1974, French police officials, describing the new breed of amateur thugs terrorizing the capital with shootouts and bursts of violence, spoke with nostalgia of the old days and the type of professional criminal found in the "Maigrets." In the past, there was an implicit understanding between crook and cop not to use a gun if at all possible. Holdups were meticulously planned and stylishly executed, and the police department had files of each criminal's tastes, habits, and compulsions. "We could put a mark on virtually every holdup," an official said. "It was like a silversmith's mark."[25] In previous years, the police could also rely on an elaborate network of informers in bars, brothels, cafés, hotels, and among concierges to keep tabs on habitual criminals, a system that has broken down in a society marked by anarchy in crime and the anonymity of criminals.

Freddie the safecracker *(Maigret et la grande perche)* belonged to the old breed of professional criminals. The police called him "Sad Freddie" and the newspapers tagged him "the burglar on a bike." Freddie had once worked for a safe manufacturing firm, but, now in business for himself, he cracked the safes he had once installed. Maigret had always felt a certain affection for Freddie, whose career he had followed for years, and it was because of this that Freddie's wife came to Maigret for help when her husband came across a dead body on one of his routine safe-cracking jobs. By solving the murder, Maigret, a policeman, permits Freddie to realize his dream and retire to the country on stolen money.

IX *Maigret's Refusal to Judge*

Maigret is employed by society to arrest the criminal, not to judge him. Simenon explained why he transmitted his own attitudes to Maigret:

I have maintained excellent contacts with the Paris Police Judiciaire: many commissaires have told me their stories. Do you know that when a criminal finally confesses after hours of interrogation, he doesn't feel humiliated, but, on the contrary, liberated? . . . [The criminal] is relieved and thanks the commissaire, he is grateful to him. Links are forged between the policeman and the guilty party. When the guillotine still existed, one-third of the condemned asked the commissaire to come to the execution. It is this link that was forged between them that represents liberty. I am sure that when . . . doctors remove the weight of a hallucination from a sick person, he must also have this feeling of deliverance, this gratitude.[26]

In Simenon's opinion, the worst humiliation for a man is to feel rejected by human society. Maigret represents a forgiving society, identifies with the criminal, and, by understanding him, gives him back his self-respect after the confession, permitting him to a certain degree to be reintegrated into the community.[27]

When Maigret has finally helped the criminal to effect a catharsis through confession, he must turn him over to the judicial process and the insensitivity of judges and juries. Simenon has often expressed his dismay at the "archaic quality of the French Penal Code, with laws that take no heed of our medical knowledge, particularly in the matter of the degree of responsibility of the criminal," adding that the first "Maigrets" were "imbued with the sense, which has always been with me, of man's irresponsibility. It is because of this feeling that Maigret does not judge, but attempts to understand."[28] Maigret separates unconditionally the policeman's job from that of the judiciary. "In any event, our role has never been to judge. It is the business of the courts and juries to decide whether a man is guilty or not and to what extent he can be considered responsible. . . . But the fact remains that there is a moment in which we must make a decision fraught with consequences . . . for, in the end, it is according to our investigation, from the elements that we have put together, that the magistrates, then the jurors, will form an opinion."[29]

Maigret's relationship with examining magistrates, the personification of abstract justice, is one of hostility. In *Une Con-*

fidence de Maigret, the commissaire explains: "Comméliau is not a bad man. He has been called my personal enemy because we have clashed at times. In reality, it's not his fault. It is a result of the idea he has of his function, of his duty. In his eyes, since he is paid by society, he must show no pity for anything that threatens to disturb the established order. Serenely, he separates the good from the bad, incapable of imagining that some can be placed in a middle ground."[30]

In order to emphasize the irrelevance of everything that occurs once the dialogue between Maigret and the criminal has ended, Simenon takes Maigret to court only once *(Maigret aux assises)* to follow up a case in which he was involved. Maigret would have preferred to remain apart from these last rites to which he has never become accustomed and which depress and discourage him.

> In his office on the Quai des Orfèvres, he was still at grips with reality, and, even when he was drawing up his report, he could still believe that his sentences stuck close to reality.
>
> Then months passed, sometimes a year, if not two, and he found himself closed in the witness room one fine day with people he had questioned formerly and who were no longer anything but a memory for him. Were these really the same human beings, concierges, passers-by, merchants, who were seated with empty expressions on the benches of the sacristy?
>
> Was it the same way, after months of prison, at the prisoner's bar?
>
> Suddenly you are plunged into an impersonal universe where everyday words no longer seem to be used, where the most ordinary facts are expressed by hermetic formulae. . . . Even today, he knew that he was giving only a lifeless, schematic reflection of reality. Everything he had just said was true, but he had not made the weight of things felt, their density, their movement, their odor. . . . Everything was falsified here, not through the fault of the judges, the jurors, the witnesses, the penal code or the procedure, but because complicated, living human beings suddenly were summed up in a few sentences.[31]

Maigret reflects that he is given only a short period in which to penetrate a new milieu, to hear ten to fifty people about whom he had previously known nothing and then, if possible, to distinguish truth from falsehood. He is continually reproached for doing the work of his men, leaving his office and going out to visit the scene of the crime, but this is indispensable for an understanding of the crime. The examining magistrate is at an even greater disadvantage, for he sees the accused only in the neutral atmosphere of his office, where they are reduced to two dimensional beings detached from their private lives. Maigret wonders what the magistrate can discover in this very limited time. After that, in court, the matter is presented in a few strokes, and the only admissible evidence is impersonal.

As he sits in court, Maigret's discouragement grows. He has been called upon to give testimony in the case of a young man named Meurant who has been accused of the murder of his aunt and a four year old child. The aunt's throat had been cut, the child suffocated, and the gold that had been kept in the bottom of a Chinese vase had disappeared. Gaston Meurant, the accused, had visited his aunt regularly, while his brother Alfred, a ne'er-do-well, came only when he needed money. Responding to an anonymous telephone tip, Maigret had found Gaston's jacket covered with blood.

Maigret knows that Meurant is innocent despite all the circumstantial evidence against him. Meurant has always wanted a family, but his wife deceived him by marrying him without telling him that she was unable to bear children. Maigret had seen men, in appearance as calm, sweet, and self-effacing as Meurant, who became violent when driven too far. However, he knows that a man like Meurant, who loved children as much as Maigret, and who also suffered because he had none of his own, would never have killed a child.

Maigret secures Meurant's acquittal and follows him to the apartment of his wife's lover, whom Meurant kills, taking justice into his own hands with Maigret's complicity. This abrogation of legal justice is not the only way in which the novel differs from the conventional detective story. The atrocity of the murder of an old woman and a four year old child, the blood stains on Meurant's suit jacket, and the activities of Meurant's brother would have been of prime importance in a typical mystery novel. Here, they are incidental to the examination of the life and character of Meurant, a man who would have preferred to be unjustly convicted of murder rather than to have the failure of his domestic life revealed in public.

Simenon's preoccupation with the imperfection of the French judicial system and the weakness of the judicial process is not limited to the "Maigrets." In *Les Témoins* he deals with it in even greater depth. Judge Lhomond has been called to the bench in the case of a man who probably killed his sluttish wife. As in most cases, there is a certain amount of doubt. By chance, at the very moment at which the trial is taking place, incidents occur in Lhomond's life that could conceivably give the impression that, were his invalid wife to die, her death could be attributed to him. It is well known that Lhomond's marriage is abominable, and that his wife has devoted herself single-mindedly to making his life miserable. The night before the opening of the trial, she broke her bottle of medicine, perhaps intentionally, and sent Lhomond out to renew the prescription. He went into a bar to telephone the pharmacist, whose night bell was out of order, and met one of his colleagues on his way out. That morning, contrary to his custom, he took a drink before coming to court because he had a bad cold. For a few moments, Lhomond was tempted to offer an explanation to his colleagues about the odor of liquor on his breath, but remained silent because he realized that they, like most people, instinctively distrusted such simple explanations. What would happen, he wondered, if his wife were to die. The doctor would be called as a witness and would remember that Lhomond had once asked him if too strong a dose of medicine could be dangerous because of the strychnine it contained, while the pharmacist would surely recall that Lhomond had awakened him in the middle of the night to renew a prescription he had just filled.

As he reflects on his own life and as he listens to the witnesses in court, the judge begins to put himself in the place of the accused. He is struck by the sudden realization of the impossibility of one human being's understanding another. And yet, it is necessary to satisfy the demands of judges and jurors who, no matter where, require clear-cut cases. While it seems doubtful, Lhomond reflects, it is possible that Lambert is innocent. When he points out to the jurors how much doubt remains, they acquit Lambert, who is as surprised by the verdict as the rest of the court. The judge is overcome by a feeling of panic when he realizes the narrow thread on which such decisions hang, for Lambert would surely have been convicted were it not for Lhomond's state of mind during the trial.

X   *A Bourgeois Hero*

While the detective novel, in general, has remained faithful to the original concept of the detective as a heroic figure, Simenon's works emphasize Maigret's simplicity and bourgeois characteristics. "I don't believe in heroes," Simenon stated. "Heroic deeds are by chance. When I was a boy, I rescued my younger brother from drowning in the flooded Meuse. Every yard further I swam, I thought: If I don't catch him the next yard, I'll turn back. It was pure chance I did not. The hero is the person who has the courage to make a good thing of his life."[32]

Maigret was all wrong for the classic fictional detective; a professional policeman, not an amateur detective, corpulent, happily married, middle-aged. Simenon writes: "When I wanted to create a sympathetic person who understood everything, that is to say Maigret, I gave him without realizing it certain of my father's characteristics."[33] Maigret, like Désiré Simenon, loves his fellow men, understands, and pities them. He knows that they have killed because they are weak or unhappy, because they feel threatened, because they are frightened. The closer he gets to his prey, the greater his sympathy because he understands him better. In an interview with Parinaud, Simenon said: "If you succeed little by little in interesting yourself [in a man] you will necessarily come to love him. I never met anyone, no matter how unattractive he may seem at first sight, whom I did not finally like after having studied him. . . . It seems to me that if men do not like one another it is through lack of knowledge and above all, because of fear. We detest what we are afraid of . . . if then, we attain knowledge, hatred is no longer possible. We are not afraid of what we know."[34]

Maigret, like Désiré, is in harmony with the world around him. His senses are acute and each of his cases is intimately linked with both his sensory impressions and the weather. The beauty of the spring day on which *Maigret et les vieillards* opens makes Maigret feel both light-hearted and melancholy, preparing one for the ambivalent mood of the novel. "It was one of those exceptional months of May such as one experiences only two or three times in a lifetime and which have the brightness, taste, and smell of childhood memories. Maigret called it a hymnal month of May because it reminded him both of his First Communion and of his first spring in Paris, when everything was new and wonderful for him. In the street, on the bus, in his office, he would stop short, struck by a sound in the distance, by a puff of warm air, by the bright spot of a dress that took him back twenty or thirty years."[35]

Intimate notations and details scattered throughout the Maigret cycle make him a completely believable human being. In *Les Mémoires de Maigret*, we learn that Maigret's father was the bailiff at the château of the count of Saint-Hilaire in Saint-Fiacre. His humble origins account for his sympathy for the little people and his attitude toward the rich. Maigret returns to his native village thirty years later, in *L'Affaire Saint-Fiacre*, when he comes across an anonymous note stating that a crime will be committed during the first mass on All Souls' Day at the Saint-Fiacre church. The police at Moulins who received it had thought it a joke, as did the Paris police to whom they forwarded it. Because they did not know Maigret's background, his fellow officers were surprised to see him act on the basis of such a note. In Saint-Fiacre, Maigret finds that the whole world of his childhood has deteriorated. The countess is a crazy old lady who keeps gigolos, and her son, a good-for-nothing playboy, is about to be arrested on a bad check charge. "He certainly had no illusions about mankind. But he was furious that his childhood memories should have been sullied! Especially the one of the countess, whom he had always seen as noble and beautiful, like a storybook character."[36]

When the first mass ends, Maigret notices that the countess is immobile and when he approaches her, he realizes that she is dead. In her missal, he finds a phony newspaper article stating that her son had committed suicide after publicly announcing that he was ashamed of the scandals provoked by his mother. The article had obviously been planted by someone who knew of her heart condition and counted on the article to bring on an attack. "Maigret felt personally attacked by the case, sick at heart, disgusted. . . . He had never imagined that he would find his native village in this condition."[37] Maigret's indignation is another quality that sets him apart from the traditional detective, for, unlike the latter, he is never coldly removed from the case at hand. Each one becomes a personal matter to him; his emotions set the mood of the novel.

The murder is solved, but not by Maigret. It is her son who redeems himself by discovering that the bailiff and his son had been robbing the countess of her money and property and had killed her when they feared her new gigolo would get in their way. At the funeral, Maigret's eyes meet those of the count. "It seemed to him that there was the shadow of a smile on Saint-Fiacre's lips. Not the smile of the sceptical Parisian, or the ruined society man. A serene, confident smile. . . ."[38]

Maigret's early years in Paris, his courtship and marriage, and his life in the police department are dealt with in detail in *Les Mémoires de Maigret*. He describes his various assignments in the streets of Paris, the central market, the docks, the crowds, the department stores, the brothels that preceded his promotion to the special brigade. Maigret's physical appearance is established in the first of the series, *Pietr-le-Letton*:

He did not resemble the ordinary policeman. He did not have a mustache nor did he wear heavy soled shoes. His clothes were well cut, of fine wool. He also shaved every morning and his hands were well groomed.

His build was plebian. He was enormous and bony. Hard muscles stood out beneath his jacket. . . . Above all, he had his very own way of planting himself in a spot that had even displeased many of his colleagues.

It was more than self-assurance, but it wasn't pride. He was like a solid block and everything had to break against it. . . . His pipe remained clenched in his jaw.[39]

Notations of Maigret's physical strength and infinite curiosity about people and things abound in the series. There emerges from all of this a picture of a quiet, unexcitable man who detests hurry, a stolid, peaceable figure who inspires confidence.

Simenon returns repeatedly to other elements that have become part of the Maigret legend; his pipe, heavy overcoat, the bowler hat he discards later on, his cherished pot-bellied stove in his office on the Quai des Orfèvres, and the all night sessions in his office, interrupted by countless trays of sandwiches and beer ordered from the Brasserie Dauphine. "Those nights, which eight times out of ten ended with confessions, had finally acquired their rules, even their traditions, like plays that are performed several hundred times."[40] Maigret's associates, carefully differentiated, make up a continually reappearing cast of characters. Among them are Janvier, the faithful, devoted to his wife and ever increasing brood of children; Torrence, who, although killed in *Pietr-le-Letton*, returns to help Maigret in subsequent investigations; Lapointe, the youngest, who can pass for a student and who is always sent out to interview middle-aged, maternal women; Lucas, the associate with the greatest ability, whose only problem is that his profession is written all over his face; Lognon, whom certain people call "Inspector Ungracious" because of his cranky air, but whom Maigret refers to as "Inspector Unfortunate" because he seems to have a gift for bringing misfortune on himself; Inspector Fumal, whose lack of formal education stands in the way of promotion; Dr. Paul, the police surgeon; and Moers, the ballistics expert. Equally familiar is Madame Maigret, who represents Simenon's concept of the ideal woman.[41] She is completely devoted to Maigret. She is an expert cook and can prepare Maigret's favorite dishes better than any chef.[42] Maigret knows that he can come home at any hour and find his wife prepared to kiss him and serve him some remarkable dish. She is satisfied with his mere presence. Roger Stéphane has remarked that there is something both medieval and touching in this relationship, one that Simenon would have wanted for his parents.[43] Madame Maigret, Maigret's life, his staff, his friends, his gourmandise, his sorrow at being childless, his constant head colds, all contribute to make him a completely believable human being.

Maigret is one of the few harmonious characters in all of Simenon's work. He is wise and kind. He knows that it is impossible to understand men completely, but he accepts them as they are. He is astonished by nothing and never moralizes. His wisdom restores faith in life. It is his reassuring presence that constitutes the major difference between the "Maigrets" and Simenon's other novels. Many of the same themes are repeated in both types of novel, and Simenon often takes up subjects in the "Maigrets" that are more serious than those in his other novels. Despite this, in the "Maigrets" Simenon only takes us to the threshold of tragedy, which he crosses in the others. This is due to the reassuring presence of Maigret, the father figure, who convinces us that there is an order, a structure, and a meaning to life. In the other novels, there is no Maigret to whom the protagonist can confess, there is no one to understand or with whom to communicate, leaving him immured in his solitude, stifled and suffocated by repressed confessions.

CHAPTER 3

Basic Themes in Simenon's Novels

I Simenon's Psychological Novels

ALL of Simenon's novels are built around psychological investigations. While, in the "Maigrets" they are carried out by the detective, in the others they are effected by the novelist rather than his alter ego. In the "Maigrets" Simenon observes the characters from a distance at first and then slowly closes in, while in the others he focuses directly on a character from the beginning and then delves deeper and deeper into his psyche to reveal what neither he nor the reader suspected previously. In the "Maigrets," Simenon starts with a given situation that he examines in order to discover the psychological imperatives behind it; in the other novels, he gradually builds up the pressures leading to the final tragedy. In none of his work, however, does Simenon attempt to provide answers to the problems he presents. Answers, he maintains, are a function of intelligence, and his tool is intuition, not intelligence.[1] While the role of intelligence is to explain, reform, justify, propose solutions, the role of intuition is to attempt to understand and, through understanding, sympathize, the only true means of communication for Simenon.

In *Quand j'étais vieux*, Simenon wrote: "Like the great naturalists, I would like to focus on certain human mechanisms. Not on great passions. Not on questions of ethics or morality. Only to study the minor machinery which may appear secondary."[2] There are certain of these "mechanisms" for which Simenon shows a predilection and which inspire certain basic themes in his work. Through an analysis of these themes as they appear and reappear, with infinite variations and subtle modifications, we may attempt to understand this vast work, one in which an enormous cast of virtually interchangeable characters acts out certain dramas in a series of extremely varied settings.

II *The Clan*

One of the essential themes in Simenon's work is that of the clan. While the clan provides a defense against solitude, it often exerts a destructive, stifling influence, particularly when dominated by the female, compelling the young man to escape its domination. "In *Je me souviens*," Simenon wrote, "I tried to give an idea of the Brüll clan and the Simenon clan. Though I revolted against both, there is no doubt that I remained marked by them."[3]

Madame Pontreau, the cold and domineering woman who runs the lives of her three daughters and son-in-law *(Le Haut Mal)*, kills her son-in-law by pushing him from the hay loft during one of his epileptic seizures. The discovery of their mother's crime has a devastating effect on her daughters: the widowed daughter commits suicide, the youngest runs off with her lover, and the oldest remains with her mother with all initiative and will destroyed.

In *Les Demoiselles de Concarneau*, Jules Guérec lives with his sisters, who adore him, attend to his every need, and protect him while sapping his mental and moral strength at the same time. When he kills a child in a hit-and-run accident, he tries to make a new life for himself with the unsuspecting mother of the dead child, but his sisters reveal the truth to her to prevent his escape. She gladly accepts the money they offer, and Jules returns, stifling any ill feeling, because "the three of them were condemned henceforth to live together."[4] He is drained of all emotion except dread at the thought that his sisters will die one day and leave him to his own resources.

The circle referred to in *Le Cercle des Mahé* is the circle of incomprehension formed by the oppressive clan from which Mahé must escape. "They had made a doctor of him. He had studied docilely all they had given him to study. Then he had permitted himself to be shut up into this grey house which they pretended was his henceforth. . . . He had not reacted. . . . They repeated to him: 'It's *your* church . . . *your* village . . . *your* friends. . . .' All of that was set up around him as if to close him up within a sacred, impassable circle. . . . He was a Mahé. As a Mahé, and because so many Mahé had been incrusted in the region, they got together to prevent him from escaping."[5] Mahé finally escapes by committing suicide. As he is drowning, his arms push back the water in circular motions as he had attempted to push back the Mahé circle.

There is only one clan in all of Simenon's work that exerts a constructive influence. Significantly, it is dominated by a strong patriarch. Omer Petermans of *Le Clan des Ostendais*, one of the few memorable characters in Simenon's novels, holds his family together under conditions of stress. Because of his strength, the clan maintains its cohesiveness, despite the disasters provoked by the German occupation that threaten to destroy it. Although many of Simenon's novels were produced during and after the Second World War, this novel and *Le Train* are the only two set against a background of war. This is because of Simenon's disinterest in politics, war, or religion.

Le Clan des Ostendais begins on a Sunday morning in May 1940, "a bright, absolutely calm morning. A smooth sea beneath a sky of irridescent blue. The world, by its tints, resembled the interior of a seashell."[6] This is the beautiful spring of the fall of Belgium and France. "The weather had never been as radiant for weeks on end. There was not a cloud in the sky, not a ripple on the sea, and the thick, glossy grass in the meadows was immobile in the sunshine."[7]

The German offensive had begun two weeks before and trainloads of Belgian, Dutch, and French refugees were pouring into La Rochelle. Without prior notice, five fishing boats flying the Belgian flag appear in the harbor carrying the families of a clan of Flemish fishermen as well as the members of their crews and their families. They had been fishing in Icelandic waters when news came of the German attack on Belgium and Holland. Vivid memories of the death and destruction of the First World War aroused their determination to avoid another encounter with the Germans. Therefore, they returned to Ostend and, under the German bombardment, loaded their families and possessions onto the boats, fleeing to a destination where the Germans could not reach them. To their despair, they are forced to join all the other refugees in the area. They wonder whether it had been worth the trouble to do all that they had done,

to have made such an effort that their limbs ached and their minds were still blank from it, to have overworked the machines after abandoning a good part of the nets, come into Ostend under the shelling and the bombs to save their wives and children and even that mirror-wardrobe which was lying on the deck, wrapped in an old sail—had it been worth doing all that to fall into a situation where people didn't understand anything, where they watched you with distrust and where they looked at you from the café terraces with opera glasses, where officers who played games by firing machine guns into the air, repeated to you while taking on airs of impor-tance: "It's the law."[8]

Neither the French nor the occupying German authorities understand the strength of the leader of the clan, Omer Petermans. Nor do they realize that it is impossible to prevent him from doing what he sets out to do. Slowly, meticulously, he plans their escape, taking his boats out fishing each day so that this will be accepted procedure the day they decide to leave. He never waivers in his determination, even when three of his boats hit mines. Finally, they leave, as he had decided to do from the beginning despite stupid rules and the disorders of war. Only his wife knows that he feels like crying because he had paid such a high price for their escape and because he wonders if he really had the right to decide for all. "But he had done the essential, he had done his task as a man . . . he had done what he could do, the best he could do."[9]

Although only two of the five boats are left and only one of his three sons has survived, although he is carrying two boatloads of widows and orphans, Omer has done his duty as a man. Simenon returns continually in his work to the difficulty of maturing emotionally to become a man. Petermans is one of the rare individuals who is able to cope successfully with this difficulty and, as a result, attains the stature of a true hero. Simenon's other protagonists merge into a grey mass, barely distinguishable from one another. Unlike Petermans, it is not they who are important, but what happens to them when they are pushed to the edge of their endurance.

The action of *Le Train* also takes place in May 1940 and deals with the flight of refugees from the approaching German army.[10] Marcel, the narrator, closes his radio repair shop in Northern France to flee with his family. He feels a sense of relief at leaving his home and responsibilities. When his car is shunted off to another track, he is separated from his pregnant wife and young daughter. He finally arrives at the refugee reception center in La Rochelle, where he has an affair with Anna, a Jewish refugee whom he met on the train. Freed of all of the burdens of normal life, he is wildly happy. "It was as if I had known, when I left Fumay," Marcel states, "what I was going to find: a little circle made to measure for me, which would become my shelter and in which it was essential for me to establish myself."[11] Nevertheless, he conscientiously continues his efforts to discover the whereabouts of his wife and child, knowing that finding them will put an end to the only true passion he has known in his life. When he discovers that his wife has just given birth at the maternity home in the town of Bressuire, he sets out to join her without joy, but also without hesitation, in an almost instinctive return to the clan. "I didn't ask myself any questions. I would go to Bressuire on foot if necessary. Since I knew where Jeanne was, I had to join her. It wasn't a matter of duty, it was so natural, that I didn't hesitate for a moment." [12] Several months later Anna, who is fleeing the Gestapo, timidly seeks out Marcel at his home, but he refuses to take the risk of hiding her. She is caught and executed. "I have never been back to La Rochelle. I shall never go back," concludes the now middle-aged narrator. "I have a wife, three children, a shop in the Rue du Château." [13]

III   *The Extended Clan*

In an interview with Simenon, Parinaud remarked that the novelist shows a great deal of affection for the extended clan. Simenon agreed and stated that, in his opinion, the most effective of all such clans is the small village because "it is the coming together of a few people who live side by side as neighbors and have the same needs. You belong to the community and it is reassuring." [14] An excellent description of the communal feeling in the small village can be found in *Maigret à l'école*, which takes place in Saint-André-sur-mer where Maigret has been called to investigate the murder of Léonie, the postmistress. While everyone in the village had despised her, and many of them had good reason to kill her, they all blame the schoolmaster for the crime because he is an outsider. At Léonie's funeral, Maigret observes the close relationships among the villagers and understands the links that have bound them together.

There were three of them, all about the same age. All three were certainly over seventy-five, and behind them, as they stood in a corner, against the white wall, was a copy of the law on establishments for the sale of public beverages and on public intoxication. They held themselves more stiffly than usual, because of their black Sunday suits and starched shirts, and this lent them a certain solemnity.

It was strange to see that though their faces were wrinkled with deep furrows, their eyes, when they looked at one another, had an innocent childish expression. Each of them had a glass in his hand. The tallest of the three, who had a magnificent crop of white hair and a silky mustache, was swaying slightly, and whenever he was disposed to speak he laid a finger on the shoulder of one of his companions.

Why did Maigret suddenly imagine them in the school playground? They were just like schoolboys in their laughter and in the glances they exchanged. They had been to school together. Later in life, they had pulled the same girls into ditches and had seen one another married, attended the funerals of their respective parents, their children's weddings and the christenings of their grandchildren.

"She might almost have been my sister; my father used to tell me he didn't know how often he'd pushed her mother down under the haystack. It seems she was a hot bitch and her husband was a cuckold from start to finish."

Didn't that go far to explain the village? Behind Maigret, in another group, someone was saying:

"When he sold me that cow, I said to him: 'Look here, Victor, I know you're a thief. But don't forget we did our military service together at Montpellier, and there was that evening. . . .' "[15]

The American equivalent of the French village is what Simenon calls the "country community." The opening paragraph of *Un Nouveau dans la ville,* one of the four novels in which Simenon describes American small town life,[16] compares the town to a family when it tells of the arrival of a mysterious stranger: "He was settled in the town without his arrival having been seen by anyone and they felt an uneasiness comparable to one a family would feel upon seeing a stranger, whom no one had seen enter, sitting in a living room armchair. . . ."[17] This small Maine town near the Canadian border is one in which everything is in its place, every detail has a meaning impossible to explain to an outsider:

The hill, Elm Street, the whole neighborhood with cottages surrounded with lawns and maple trees, all that is easy to understand at first glance. You know that you will find there white collar employees, doctors, lawyers, directors and assistant directors, families with children and a cleaning woman who comes once or several times a week.

You need only draw up the list of names on the letter boxes and you know in advance the names that you will read in the newspaper on the occasion of marriages, dances, and charity bazaars.

Around the tannery, people swarm who have come from everywhere, five or six hundred men and women, certain of whom speak languages no one understands.

For twenty years, the farmers who form the base of the population and whose families for the most part have been there for several generations, have been trying to get rid of the tannery and that is the most hotly disputed matter at each election.

You hardly see these wealthy farmers and you never see them in bars, for they prefer to meet at their club, the stone building opposite the city park. In the winter, when the snow covers their land, they go in search of the sun to Florida or to California.[18]

The plot is very simple. The stranger, Ward, has betrayed certain

colleagues in the Mafia and has come to this small town to escape
their vengeance. The murderers finally find and kill him with the
help of the local bartender who fears Ward's evil influence on the
town. As in all of Simenon's novels, the plot is of secondary importance. What is of interest is the study of Ward, a man who hates
everybody. Lucid in his hatred, recognizing and accepting his own
evil tendencies, Ward discovers the vices hidden behind the facade
of decency, exposes, and exploits them. He is able to impose his will
because "absolute evil, evil incarnate in a man, is irresistible."[19]

Spencer Ashby, the outsider in *La Mort de Belle*, is a different individual from Ward, but he, too, encounters the hostility of a closely knit community at a moment of crisis. Originally from Vermont,
he settled in his wife's home town in Connecticut where he now
teaches in a prep school. When their young boarder is raped and
murdered, suspicion falls on Ashby. He begins to feel persecuted, as
even his wife appears to suspect him. The minister's Sunday sermon
seems to be directed at Ashby, who realizes that,

it was long before the sermon that he had the impression of being excluded
from the community. They didn't accuse him. They didn't stone him. They
didn't say anything to him. Had they perhaps only tolerated him all these
years? It wasn't his village. It wasn't his church. No family here knew his
family and none of his ancestors were in the cemetery, not a tomb, not a
page in the parish records bore his name. . . . It was very clear in his
mind, the two thousand or so inhabitants of the area made up a whole; they
were linked to one another, not by a vague feeling of solidarity or of duty,
but by bonds as close and as complicated as those at the base of great
families.[20]

The shock provoked by the suspicion around him makes Ashby
feel guilty, as he begins to suspect his own spiritual integrity.
"What [Dostoevsky] contributed above all, in my opinion," writes
Simenon, "is a new notion of the idea of guilt. Guilt is no longer the
simple, clearly defined matter one finds in the penal code, but
becomes a personal drama that takes place in the individual's
soul."[21] The doubt of the others becomes contagious, causing Ashby
to wonder whether he might actually have been capable of committing such a crime. He becomes obsessed with this idea and, to free
himself of this obsession, commits a sadistic crime, almost identical
to the first.

There is in small American towns what Simenon describes as a
religious and social geography.[22] Higgins, the protagonist of *La*

Boule noire, is blackballed for membership in the country club of the Connecticut town in which he and his family have lived for the past ten years.

The community had rejected him. Perhaps it wasn't completely accurate. The country club wasn't the entire community. . . . The long and short of it was that the moment had come when, after permitting and even encouraging him to forge ahead, they were telling him firmly to go no further. They were notifying him that he wasn't worth enough to belong to the community. One part of the community, granted! He could go to the Rotary luncheons and . . . parade in the American Legion uniform on the fourth of July. Only, he didn't have the right to play golf at the country club . . . [23]

Higgins becomes aware of many things that had previously escaped his notice. At a town meeting, he discovers "what he was tempted to call the geography of the room, which, besides, was only a projection of the geography of the town. He had never wondered why certain people sat in the first rows while others gathered in certain corners. It was, however, as revealing as the neighborhoods of Williamson."[24]

Higgins also discovers that he unconsciously chose his religious denomination according to his social rank.

It was he who had chosen his church, for no precise reason, and today, observing the faces and the backs around him, he thought he understood. You didn't see there the Blairs, or the Olsens, or the Hotcombs, or most of the important people, all of whom belonged to the High Presbyterian Church.

The members of the congregation here also belonged to a certain middle class, the one that struggles to climb one or two rungs in the social ladder and to have their children climb still others. Almost all had a difficult time at the beginning and they felt reassured in the austere atmosphere of their church where everything was cold and clean, without any of the pomp and ceremony of the High Church.[25]

Although he is tempted briefly to revolt against the hypocrisy of the society around him and sink back into the depths from which he had raised himself by constant effort, Higgins's final solution is the antithesis of the one chosen by Ashby. "What was important was to conform to the rules, of course, but knowing that life was a game. If you did not play the game, it made the position of others untenable."[26] Higgins decides that he will do all that he is asked to do, a decision of which he is not proud but that he recognizes to be necessary. "Was that what they called becoming a man? If so, he had remained a child until the age of forty-five."[27] He wonders whether he is like everyone else or whether there are people who are happy. "It wasn't the precise word, but he knew what he meant. There is no word for what he meant: someone who is at peace with himself and who asks no questions, or else has found the answers. . . ."[28]

Higgins's state of mind is symptomatic of that of the majority of Simenon's characters, very few of whom are at peace with themselves. For Simenon, there is no such thing as active happiness; happiness, for him, is finding a temporary state of equilibrium. Higgins's inability to find a kindred soul, Ashby's inability to convince others of his innocence, are symptomatic of the lack of communion between individuals and their resultant solitude and isolation. This theme, which Simenon has treated more than any other, as well as the theme of guilt felt by characters who are pushed to existential limits in crisis situations, places Simenon's novels in the mainstream of modern literature despite his use of traditional plot structure.

IV   *The Foreigner—Symbol of Alienation*

In many of the novels with French settings, Simenon uses foreigners to symbolize man's fundamental solitude and alienation. M. Hire *(Les Fiançailles de M. Hire)*, born in France of Russian-Jewish parents, becomes the prime suspect when a prostitute is robbed and murdered. He is literally hounded to death by an angry mob while the real murderer watches. Twenty-five years later, Simenon again takes up the character, but more fully developed, in the person of Jonas Milk *(Le Petit homme d'Arkangelsk)*. Milk, who came to France as a child and grew up there, never forgets that he is a "foreigner, a member of another race."[29] He is constantly grateful for the tepid acceptance accorded him by his neighbors and does not resent their innuendos when he marries the town slut, Gina. One evening, Gina takes off without notice on one of her periodic escapades. Certain that she will return after she has had her fling, Milk tells inquirers that she went to Bourges, adding details as the days pass in the belief that he is protecting Gina. Gina's brother, who had never liked Milk, begins circulating disturbing rumors, insinuating that Milk could very well have killed Gina and disposed of her body. These unfounded rumors come to the attention of the authorities, who decide to open an inquiry. They ask him why he had lied about his wife's being in Bourges, and why he, a Jew, had become a Catholic. As the irrelevant questions pile up, "he is no longer Monsieur Jonas, the bookseller in the square whom everybody greets cheerfully."[30] He had become a foreigner again, a man from another clan, a man from another world. He didn't deserve it, not only because he was innocent of everything they might accuse him of,

> but because he had always tried, discreetly, quietly, to live like them, with them, and to be like them. . . . He believed only a few days before that he had succeeded by dint of patience and humility. For he had been humble as well. He did not lose sight of the fact that he was a foreigner, born in far-off Archangel, whom the fortunes of war and revolution had transplanted to a small town in the Berry. . . . [Milk] had always tried to become integrated. He did not ask the people to recognize him as one of themselves. He felt that was impossible. He behaved with the discretion of a guest and it was as a guest that he saw himself.[31]

Now, Milk realizes that the others see him as a foreigner, a Jew, "a solitary, a man from the other end of the world who had come like a parasite to embed himself in the flesh of the Old Market."[32] Although a witness comes forward who saw Gina take off with her lover, Milk hangs himself because he sees that he has remained a foreigner to those among whom he has always lived. The unexpected hostility of the neighbors, who he felt were his friends, drives him to suicide.

The foreigner in the person of the little Jewish tailor appears several times in Simenon's works, but he is used to the greatest effect in *Les Fantômes du chapelier*. In two previous versions of the novel, short stories entitled *Le Petit Tailleur et le chapelier* and *Bénis soient les humbles*, the hatmaker's crimes are seen through the tailor's eyes, while the novel takes us within the character of the hatmaker himself.

M. Labbé, the hatter, had a neurotic wife who tormented him with her unreasonable, capricious demands. He finally killed her, certain that no one would notice her disappearance since she had refused to see anyone for years. After the murder, he rigged up a device that permitted him to enter a closet in his shop below and activate a mechanism to simulate the sound of his wife's knocks that had summoned him to her bedside. To complete the picture, he set one of his wooden hatter's heads on a pole near the window so that the silhouette would be visible outside through the drawn curtains. Each night, he has the maid prepare a dinner, which he then carries up to his wife's room and eats himself. However, as Christmas approaches, he remembers that his wife would alter her schedule once a year on her birthday to receive former school friends. There are still seven of them in town and M. Labbé decides to murder them. He strangles the first six, and because he has always lived in La Rochelle, has always known the same people, and followed the same routine, he is never suspected. When he enters the café, followed by the little foreign tailor whose shop is near his and who meekly follows him there each day, no one speaks to the tailor because he isn't part of the group. "He had not gone to the same schools, had not been in the same barracks. When the middle-aged card players in the café were already on intimate terms, he was living God knows where in the Near East, where people like him were transported like cattle from Armenia to Smyrna, from Smyrna to Syria, to Greece or elsewhere."[33] Labbé, on the other hand, calls everyone by his first name. "With a glance, he had seen where they were in the game. One could have said that the game had been going on for years and years, since it was resumed every day at the same time, at the same table, with the same drinks in front of the same players, the same pipes and the same cigars."[34]

The tailor sees what he thinks is a white thread on Labbé's pants, reaches out to take it off, and notes that it is a small piece of newspaper with some of the letters cut out. The tailor is panic-stricken because he knows that the murderer has been writing to the newspapers after each murder to justify his actions, using letters cut out of the paper. The tailor, who is tempted to denounce Labbé for the reward that he needs desperately, hesitates both because he is afraid of Labbé and because he feels that a foreigner would not be believed. His dilemma makes him sick with worry.

Labbé, infused with the pride of a true paranoic after the first six murders, loses his confidence when he realizes that the seventh victim, now Mother Saint-Ursula, will escape as she is not permitted to leave the convent. When he hears the habitués of the café describe the murderer as a poor, sick individual, Labbé's pride is wounded and he seeks out someone to whom he can unburden himself, someone who will understand his actions. He chooses a motherly woman who serves as rotating mistress to several of the town notables. Unable to control himself, he also kills her, thereby proving that his claims to lucidity, his belief in the necessity of his crimes, were but a screen behind which to hide his homicidal compulsions from himself. That is why he feels relief when the police come to arrest him at the scene of the last murder and why a smile of relief flickers across his lips as the handcuffs are placed on his wrists.

The hostility to the foreigner described in many of Simenon's novels becomes xenophobia in *Chez Krull*, one of his most interesting works. The setting is the familiar grocery store/bar catering to bargeowners, their families, and the carters who guide the boats. The Krull's clientele is restricted to this group, since their neighbors ostracize them because they are foreigners.

Hans Krull of the German branch of the family arrives in France seeking a comfortable haven in his aunt's home. He acts as a catalyst, stirring up the various members of the family by revealing to them their repressed tendencies, and finally provokes the suicide of his uncle, old Cornelius, the deaf basketmaker who, like Simenon's uncle Lunel, had taken refuge in his deafness. The Krull clan is menaced on the inside by Hans and on the outside by the townspeople who automatically accuse their son Joseph, a foreigner, of the rape and murder of a young girl. Although they need no encouragement, the citizens' anger is exacerbated by Hans, who continues to call attention to himself and to the Krull family. The hysteria of the mob reaches such proportions that they storm the Krull home, and the police are obliged to intervene and arrest Joseph in order to protect him. Hans is driven from the house by his aunt, who finally realizes the extent of his malevolence.

V   *The Identity of Opposites*

Chez Krull contains another theme that is important in Simenon's work, that of the "identity of opposites."[35] When Hans first arrives at the Krull's home, he sees his aunt pushing a drunken woman out of the bar as the women exchange insults. The woman, an alcoholic nicknamed Pipi, lives with her daughter and a tramp on an abandoned, partly submerged barge. Hans discovers that there is a complex relationship between Pipi and his straightlaced aunt, a "mixture of hatred and attraction, a need, at certain moments, to test their strength against one another. . . . Perhaps Pipi was as necessary to Aunt Maria as Aunt Maria was to her. Pipi would come regularly to pour out her anger. She found at the Krull's a place where, while drinking, it was permissible to vent her hatred and rancor. Aunt Maria, for her part, had a chance to sigh virtuously before such a perfect specimen of human degradation."[36] Perhaps Aunt Maria saw in Pipi a caricature of herself, what she could have become if she had not been so resolutely virtuous. Hans reflects that he resembles his cousin Joseph and that he could have been Joseph just as Aunt Maria could have been Pipi.

The premise of the identity of opposites leads to the conclusion that destinies are interchangeable, that a single event such as a serious disappointment, an unexpected meeting, or a death is sufficient to transform an existence. The theory that all destinies are governed by accident is illustrated in *L'Homme de Londres*. In this novel, Maloin, an inoffensive railroad switchman on the waterfront in Dieppe, accidentally sees one man knock another into the water with a case that he witnessed being smuggled past customs. Maloin leaves his signal cabin during the night, recovers the bag, which contains a large sum of money, and hides it in his locker. The rest of the novel deals with the effect on him of this concealment of a crime. The French and English police are soon searching for the burglar, an Englishman, who has remained in Dieppe. The thief soon notices Maloin, who seems to be following him. Maloin, with a certain sense of guilt, decides to return the money if asked to do so. By not asking for it, the Englishman changes both of their destinies. Maloin discovers the fishing cabin in which the man is hiding and goes to bring him food. The terrified fugitive misunderstands his action and attacks Maloin with a metal hook which Maloin grabs and, with an instinctive, defensive reaction, uses to kill him. "It was idiotic, but that was the ways things were! What was most revolting was that things could have been otherwise. Everything had depended on chance. For example, when Brown had almost come up to his glassed-in cabin that night and had stopped on the second step! What would they have said to one another up there? And when he followed Maloin to his house without making up his mind to talk to him, when Maloin was ready to return the suitcase! . . . What would they have said to each other? What would they have decided? What would have happened to them next?"[37]

VI   *Destruction of the Clan*

In *Chez Krull*, Simenon demonstrates that a single disruptive influence can destroy a clan. Most often in his work, the attack does not come from outside: the destruction of the clan is precipitated by the revolt of a young man against it. The flight from the family unit and the concomitant rebellion against the society it represents is common to all of Simenon's young men. Their revolt represents a passionate refusal to accept a limited, mediocre life and the monotony and ugliness of the existence they see around them. Like Roger *(Pedigree)*, they are torn between their desire for conformity and tradition, which Simenon terms order, and their individualistic tendencies. Simenon wrote in *Quand j'étais vieux:* "I am against every established order, against every imposed discipline. But I cannot live without order and discipline. . . . Protective instinct? It's possible, for I may have just missed becoming a Bohemian." [38]

Simenon's young men know what they have to do and violently oppose anything that stands in their way. It is almost as if they were destined for revolt from birth. Only in this respect do they differ from an even larger group of middle-aged men whose revolt comes later on in life, after they have spent years living according to the rules of society.

VII   *Revolt and Violence*

The acts of violence that conclude so many of Simenon's novels are, to him, "tragic consequences of the fact that for many men and women life is sometimes, if not nearly always, unendurable. In the moment of crisis, they are driven to affirm themselves and, human society being what it is, they can affirm themselves only through murder, rape, arson, suicide, and the rest of the catalogue of crimes." [39]

From the very beginning of *Faubourg*, the reader knows that the protagonist is violent and will commit a crime of violence. Driven by strange compulsions he does not himself understand, De Ritter returns to the town he left more than twenty years before, accompanied by a young prostitute named Léa. De Ritter had fled the meanness and pettiness he saw around him as well as a family that seemed to be composed only of people who were sick, unhappy, alcoholics, or crazy. He had intended to spend only a short time in the town, but suddenly and unexpectedly he decides to stay. But this desire, like all his desires, is only temporary for he has never really known what he wants. As soon as he succeeds in marrying his rich, adoring cousin, he becomes uneasy because "he [is] a victim . . . he would have been a good little boy if life had not taken it upon itself to fling him into adventure." [40] He becomes jealous of

Léa, whom he has forbidden to leave town. Finally, he kills the eighteen year old schoolboy who is infatuated with her, thereby giving in to the act of violence that has always been his destiny.

La Veuve Couderc, like *Faubourg*, builds up inexorably to murder. Just before the novel begins, the doors of Fontevrault prison opened for Jean Passerat-Monnoyeur after five years. Since then, he had been "walking straight ahead, aimlessly, he had had no more ties, everything had been a free gift, the days no longer counted, nothing counted except the magnificent present humming with sunshine."[41] As he walks along a country road, a bus returning from market stops beside him and he boards it. Widow Couderc, who is on the bus, needs a man around her farm and takes him home with her. He lives some of the happiest hours of his life there, "uncovenanted hours, hours he had not reckoned on, and his head was full of light, his nostrils drunk with summer scents, his limbs heavy with peace."[42] But he is unable to escape his past which, as in all of Simenon's novels, weighs heavily on the present and determines the relentless march toward the future.

Jean was the neglected son of a wealthy, promiscuous man. When he was fourteen years old, his English teacher picked on him because he was jealous of Jean's father. As a result, he stayed away from school, deprived of discipline as well as of love. He began to emulate his father's dissolute life. One day, when he had lost a considerable amount at cards, he followed the winner and asked him to return his money. When the man refused, Jean hit him with brass knuckles, stole his wallet, and then, after a while, threw the prostrate man off the bridge into the water. Before he committed the murder, he told himself to stop. And "if he had not done so, was it not precisely because he wanted to be done with it all? Was it not because he was sick at heart, because he had had enough?"[43] His crime was motivated by a desire for suicide.

Jean becomes the lover of the widow's niece of whom she is intensely jealous and realizes that all he did to escape was in vain. "It would start all over again—real life, complications, and, as always, he would be the one to bear the brunt of fate. He was sure of it. . . . He was dreadfully tired. Not only because of the past, or the present, but because of all the complications he could foresee."[44] He had just thrown away the innocent peace he had known only twice in his life, once when he was ill and had ceased to think about school, and again there, on the farm, before complications set in. He knew that he would never again find such peace. "Always that vague sensation of disquiet, even of anguish. He looked around him as if wondering from which quarter the blow would fall on him."[45]

The widow begs him not to see her niece. When she falls at his feet, he can bear it no longer. He takes a hammer and kills her. "What good would it be?" he thinks. "It would only start all over again! And then again, and again! He had had enough."[46] His final words, as the police come to arrest him, "I'm tired. . . . I'm so tired,"[47] express his infinite weariness.

Maudet *(L'Aîné des Ferchaux)* is another impatient young man, "impatient to live, to enjoy to the full everything life has to offer. But, above all, impatient to dominate."[48] Maudet's childhood had been impossible, and he had sworn to escape the mediocrity he saw all around him. When he hears that a certain Dieudonné needs a secretary for a well-paying, glamorous position involving travel, Maudet, who is down on his luck in Paris, convinces his young wife to accompany him to Caen to apply for this position.

In a short prologue to the novel, Simenon tells the story of the two Ferchaux brothers, Dieudonné and Emile, who had made their fortune in Africa in the 1890s. Emile, the younger brother, returned to enjoy his fortune in Paris, while Dieudonné remained in Africa, where a legend grew up around him. As his power and fortune increased, his reputation became more and more loathsome. It was known that he had native wives in every African village he visited and that he forced himself on the wives of his white employees. It was also known that he had once killed three of his bearers with a charge of dynamite when they threatened to desert him. All of this was accepted practice in colonial possessions until 1934, when legal action was taken against the Ferchaux brothers at the request of a minor government official who was thought to be the instrument of more powerful interests. A scandal, rivaling the Panama Canal scandal, had broken and Dieudonné returned to France to defend himself. It is at this point that the novel opens as Maudet and his wife leave Paris for Caen.

From their very first meeting, Ferchaux and Maudet are drawn to one another, for reasons that become clearer as the novel progresses. Ferchaux finds in Maudet a strength almost equal to the one that helped him overcome almost insuperable odds in his youth, while Ferchaux personifies for the younger man the power and riches he hopes to obtain. Anne Richter has observed that they are also drawn together by the magnetic force of destiny; they need one another and each one feels instinctively that the other will serve as the instrument of his destiny.[49] She adds that this couple represents one of the strangest attempts made by Simenon's heroes to conjure death, for, by uniting, they are struggling against a type of extinction, "for the young man, death by suffocation in a mediocre and absurd life, for the old man, sinking into the implacable exile of solitude."[50]

At first, Maudet admires everything about Ferchaux. With the reverence of a Candide, he notes that boredom explains Ferchaux's scorn for most people and things, "an immense, icy boredom, the boredom of a man who has seen everything, known everything, who has lost all his illusions and who finally knows how infinite is human solitude. That boredom would have been the same in a Parisian mansion as in the house on the dunes."[51] What Maudet does not realize at first is that Ferchaux's glory belongs to the past, that he can go no further. A reversal in roles between master and disciple occurs when Maudet discovers this and understands that Ferchaux is afraid of being alone.

The study of the relationship between the two is interwoven with an exciting adventure story. Maudet and Ferchaux flee with Maudet's wife from Caen to Dunkirk and, as the police close in on them, they abandon her and sail for South America. The second part of the novel takes place in Panama where the two men have settled. Ferchaux is old and sick. He is busy dictating his memoirs, afraid that he will not have enough time to finish them. It is only since he began them that he has become so frightened of death. Maudet, who is becoming more and more disgusted with the old man, is growing restless. Constantly straining toward the future, Maudet realizes that "his contact with people and things could only last as long as was necessary to draw out their substance, as it were. When there was nothing else to take, it was necessary to move on."[52] That was why he had abandoned Lina and that is why Ferchaux must now disappear. He has lived too long with Ferchaux and there is nothing else to take from him but his money. "He was forced to follow his path as Ferchaux had followed his. It was Ferchaux who had taught this to him when he told him the story of the three blacks he had been obliged to kill. It was a necessity, a duty."[53]

At times Maudet would have a certain feeling that would let him know that what had to be done would be done. "It was when he felt removed from the surroundings in which he found himself, as if in a dream."[54] One day this occurs and Maudet listens attentively as Jef, the bartender, tells him that during westerly gales, headless bodies of old people are frequently washed up on the beach. This is the work of the sellers of shrunken heads. Jef explains that white heads sell better than colored heads and heads of old people are in great demand because they have more expression and also dry faster.

One rainy night, Maudet performs the necessary act, assassinating the old man with hammer blows and knife thrusts, but he leaves the body for the old drunken seller of shrunken heads to complete the job while he takes off for an unknown destination. Although he steals all of Ferchaux's money, Maudet's motivation was not solely theft, for he also had a desire for freedom to complete his journey to the limits of his possibilities.[55] Four years later, he appears in Singapore where he goes under the name of Captain Philps. He is young, slim, sunburned, dances perfectly, and drinks heavily. Despite his chronological age, his hair is slightly grey at the temples and there is unfathomable irony in his smile, a fixity in his eyes which belie his conviviality. He has a way of saying jocularly—at least those to whom he addresses himself take it as such and protest vehemently: " 'I'm really quite old.' It gives him particular pleasure to be the only one to know that he is right."[56]

Frank Friedmaier's childhood *(La Neige était sale)* was even more sordid and tragic than Maudet's. He grew up in his mother's brothel in an unnamed Central European country, which is now occupied by the Germans. While most of the population is freezing and starving, Lotte Friedmaier is well supplied by her German customers. Frank is disgusted with himself and with the life he is leading and turns to crime as a way of avenging himself on a world that did not permit him to remain pure. Motivated by cold, defiant despair, he gratuitously kills a German soldier. When the young violinist upstairs is arrested for the crime, Frank knows that his old mother will die of grief, but he feels no pity, "not for anybody. Not even for himself. He neither asked for pity nor would he accept it,"[57] and that was why he was so irritated with Lotte; she gazed fondly at him, her eyes full of anxiety and tenderness.

Frank feels no pity either when he murders an old woman, who had been kind to him when he was a child, in order to steal watches for a German general. His most abominable crime, however, is perpetrated against Sissy Holst, the daughter of their next door neighbor. Holst, an intellectual reputed to be in the resistance, is now an impoverished bus driver. Frank is drawn magnetically to Holst, who represents the father he never had. Because of his need to defile everything in order to externalize his infinite self-hatred, Frank lures Sissy, who loves him, into his bed. As prearranged, he changes places in the darkness with his friend, Fred Kromer, a bully, thief, and murderer. The plot misfires and Sissy runs out into the snow barefoot, screaming Frank's name. "It did not matter. Frank had done what he wanted to do. He had rounded the cape. He had seen what was on the other side. He had not seen what he expected to see. No matter . . . he was on the other side of the turning and he had nothing in common with them any more."[58]

Sissy is found and brought home by her father and the scandal is hushed up, but Frank is seized by a mania to court danger. "He wanted fate to take notice of him. He had done everything possible to force it to do so, and he continued to challenge it from morning to night. . . . Fate was lying in wait for him somewhere. But where? Instead of waiting for fate to reveal itself at its appointed time, Frank ran after it, casting about everywhere in his search."[59] One morning, without warning, "fate gives him a gift."[60] He is arrested by the Germans for crimes that he did not commit and locked up in a former school converted into a prison. He realizes that he has made progress since leaving his milieu, while his mother and those around her continue to live and think in the same way as before, so that they never progress. He thinks of Holst and understands that he has always admired him and resolves to remain silent in order to become worthy of him. When his mother visits him, he rejects her and asks to see Holst instead. To secure Holst's visit, Frank must reveal to the Germans certain information he had previously withheld.

Holst comes to see him in prison, bringing Sissy with him, and, with a simple gesture, he brings Frank peace, for this gesture wipes out all sin. Holst places his hand on Frank's shoulder, "exactly as Frank always thought a father would do."[61] By this action, Holst becomes a father to Frank and, like Désiré, like Maigret, he brings the paternal pardon that wipes out solitude. Before he turns away, Holst pronounces the words that express a recurring theme in Simenon's work: "It's a difficult job to be a man."[62]

Frank and Sissy look at one another. "There were no rings. There was no key. Nor were there any prayers, but Holst's words took their place. . . . He would have had only that. That was his whole share. There was nothing before and there is nothing afterward. That was his wedding! This was his honeymoon, it was his whole life that he had to live compressed into a single moment. . . . It is not the length of time that counts. What counts is that it had happened,"[63] that Sissy had come and that Holst had blessed them.

After their visit, Frank, at peace with his destiny, does everything possible to hasten his death, for he understands that everything has a price and that the one who does not pay his debts and rejects his responsibilities cannot become a man. Raymond has remarked that Frank embraces death as the "sublime and possibly only safe way of witnessing to a human absolute—a state of ecstasy and fulfillment."[64] As he is led away to be executed, it begins to snow and the clean snow, representing his expiation and purification, covers the dirty snow of his desperate soul.

Holst absolves Frank as Maigret absolves the criminals whom he must turn over to justice because both know that man is not master of his destiny and, therefore, is not responsible for his actions. Maigret and Holst speak for Simenon when they express the belief that there are no guilty men, only victims.[65] When he visits Frank in prison, Holst explains to him why he has come to believe this:

I had a son, a boy a little older than you. His ambition was to become a great doctor. He was passionately interested in medicine and nothing else mattered to him. When I no longer had money, he decided to continue his studies at any price.

One day, expensive products, mercury, platinum, disappeared from the physics laboratory. Then people in the university began to complain of petty thefts. Finally, a student who walked into the cloakroom saw my son steal a wallet.

He was twenty-one years old. As they were taking him to the rector's office, he jumped out of a second story window.[66]

VIII *Salvation Through Paternity*

In Simenon's work, the discovery of the father is the discovery of "virile love which exalts strength, which gives the desire to build, to found, to protect."[67] Simenon showed, in *Pedigree*, the way in which his father's illness saved him from ruining his life in debauchery. The situation is repeated in *L'Âne Rouge*, in which Cholet is sinking into vice, justifying his debasement by his superstitious belief that "it was necessary to get down to rock bottom! It was the only way to finally extricate oneself. Once at the bottom, in one way or another, it would end."[68] The miracle of salvation occurs with the death of his father. "The miracle was to gather everyone around him in this concert of infinite indulgence. .. . . It was really a liberation! Jean hiccupped, coughed, unable to catch his breath. They turned to him. A hand was placed on his shoulder. 'You must be a man.' . . . Now everyone was nice to him! They were going to put him back on the right track. The past was wiped out."[69] As the novel ends, Jean sits at the table and realizes that he has inadvertently taken his father's chair.

Interest is centered on the father figure rather than on the son in 45° à l'ombre. Donadieu, doctor on board l'Aquitaine, a ship returning to France from French Equatorial Africa, has taken notice of a young man named Huret. "He did not know why he felt more concerned about this young man than about his other passengers. Rather, he preferred not to admit the reason. It was simply an intuition that he had when he first met anyone. Not a doctor's intuition. He had had it long before he chose his profession. . . . He just sensed that certain human beings are born to catastrophe as others are born to live out a long, peaceful life. From the first moment he saw him, before he knew who Huret was or that he had a sick child, Huret's face had struck him in this way."[70]

L'Aquitaine seems to be subject to the evil eye, a malady that "attacks boats on all the seas of the world, and the causes of which belong to the great unknown domain called Chance. . . . Even if the start of the trip seems favorable, the signs of the evil eye cannot escape the sailor's eye. Suddenly, without reason, a part of the rigging breaks like a violin string. . . . Or the cabin boy cuts open his thumb. . . . It's not yet the evil eye. The evil eye requires a series. But it is rare for new damage not to follow that night or the next day. From then on, everything goes from bad to worse and the men, with clenched jaws, have only to count the blows."[71]

To a series of mechanical difficulties on the Aquitaine is added a yellow fever epidemic that breaks out in the hold. This is kept from the first class passengers, who include Huret, his wife and dying baby, an old, disreputable French colonial, a seemingly mad army medical officer, and his promiscuous wife. Donadieu is most concerned about Huret because of his premonition. When one of Donadieu's friends had once told him jokingly that he should be named "God-the-Father,"[72] he hadn't laughed. It was, indeed, a mania with him to worry about others, not in order to intervene in their lives, not to make himself important, but because he could not remain indifferent to those he saw around him sliding toward joy or catastrophe. Like Maigret, Donadieu is a "mender of destinies." Because he cannot prevent himself from being profoundly moved by the tragedies of others, he smokes opium every night in the privacy of his cabin. There, for a while, he no longer torments himself by worrying about all those who, in any event, cannot escape their destiny. In this novel, as in all of Simenon's work, no solutions are presented for the problems posed. The characters get off the boat exactly as they were when they boarded it, taking their anxieties and frustrations along with them.

The theme of the father as friend and mentor, possessing the power to exorcize evil and despair, is developed throughout Simenon's work. Simenon once stated that he noticed that most men have more memories of their father than of their mother, and that paternal love was almost always stronger than maternal love. He added that many women don't know what maternal love is, a feeling shared by most doctors and policemen.[73]

Le Fils is a confession in the form of a long letter written by Alain Lefrançois to his sixteen year old son, Jean-Paul, "a Lefrançois, as my father and his father before him were Lefrançois. It's the same family that continues and in which, almost without being aware of it, you change places."[74] Lefrançois had decided to write this letter at his father's funeral so that his son would understand why he venerated his father. He cautions Jean-Paul, who had looked upon his grandfather with a certain amount of scorn, against the danger of judging people by superficial appearances. "Youth hates old people, upon whom it looks as if they were a blemish of creation. . . . Is that what I read in your eyes? If not hatred, at the very least scorn and, at the same time, ill feeling because that old man interfered by being your grandfather, your predecessor, someone whose blood is in your veins and to whom you bear a resemblance, whether you want to or not."[75]

Now that Jean-Paul is no longer a child, Lefrançois feels that he will be able to understand the tragedy that took place in 1928 when he was nineteen years old and that ruined the life of Jean-Paul's grandfather, at that time prefect of the Charentes-Maritime. When Lefrançois's young mistress became pregnant, he caused her death by a clumsily induced abortion. To save his son, the prefect declared that he was guilty, exchanging a promising career for five years in prison.

Alain Lefrançois warns his son of the danger of judging summarily not only his grandfather, but anyone else. The senile, deformed grandmother Jean-Paul had known was once young and witty, and Jean-Paul's mother had not always been the authoritarian, superficial woman she appeared to be. During the war, she had risked deportation and death for her activities in the Resistance. Paradoxically, those had probably been the best years of her life because she had found a field of action to her measure. "Each one of us needs to be aware of his importance,"[76] Lefrançois continues, echoing an idea that explains most of Simenon's work. In *Le Roman de l'homme,* Simenon wrote that one of the causes of the malaise of our period is the fact that people cannot maintain any illusions about their own worth. An artisan is proud of his professional ability, a country housewife is certain that she makes the best soup in the village, while the interchangeable factory or office worker can only find satisfaction elsewhere, if he ever does find it.[77] It is because Simenon devotes his novels to these interchangeable people that there are so few memorable characters in his work. It also explains in part Simenon's great appeal, since it is easy for the reader to identify with his characters and to empathize with their inarticulate longings, their desperate desire to be something other than a cog in a machine.

IX   *A Man is Complete Only in the Third Generation*

Just as Alain Lefrançois's father fulfilled the paternal role of protector, Alain, by writing the letter to his son, is fulfilling the role of the son, which is to serve as witness for his father. Simenon believes that a man lives his life out fully only in his children and grandchildren; he is complete only in the third generation. "I read that after our death we live on for about one hundred years, approximately the time it takes for those who knew us, then for those who heard about us directly from them, to disappear in their turn. Then it is oblivion, or legend. . . . One hundred years! Three generations! Look around you, question your friends. You will realize that, with a few rare exceptions, these three generations represent the limits of survival. And this survival is dependent on the original testimony, that of the son."[78]

It is the despair of the witness that causes the ultimate tragedy in *Les Quatre jours du pauvre homme,* one of the most poignant of Simenon's novels. The four days of the title cover the two turning points in the life of François Lecoin. During the first two days, he is presented as a slightly honest but respectable failure. He does not realize at the time that he is happy, despite his poverty, because he has the friendship and trust of his son, Bob. The events of the third and fourth days take place three years later when Lecoin has achieved financial success as the owner of a blackmailing sheet, *La Cravache*. His son is now studying at the Lycée Stanislas with the sons of the richest families in Paris. However, Lecoin has overreached himself by blackmailing an important finance minister, and the government has decided to suppress the paper. Lecoin reflects that this might be an opportunity sent to him by fate to start all over again, to live a worthwhile life with his son in new surroundings with different people. "It was neither fortune nor luxury that he desired, but a worthy life, and that word had a precise meaning for him which he was not capable of explaining. Not to tremble before anyone, before any man! Not to tremble before life! Not to feel that he was an inferior being to whom other beings assigned limits according to their interest or their whims. Not to have to cheat, to lie, even to himself!"[79]

But fate does not provide such opportunities to start over again. In Simenon's universe, one is condemned to a destiny that does not change; one does not start over again, one continues. Lecoin becomes aware of this when his son, learning the source of his father's income, hangs himself. When he had his son, Lecoin had thought that he was the most unfortunate of men. After Bob's suicide, Lecoin almost feels like "smiling indulgently at the imbecile he had been who understood nothing and who had gone so far to discover such simple truths. How he had struggled! All his life he had flailed around ineffectually, he had run obstinately from one wall to another without finding a way out."[80] As the novel ends, Lecoin decides to turn himself in rather than commit suicide, so that his dead son will understand that it is all over.

Dave Galloway *(L'Horloger d'Everton)* belongs to the same breed of men as Lecoin. "It seemed to him that, in the whole world, there were only two sorts of men, those who bowed their heads and the others. As a child, he had already thought it in more literal terms, the spanked and those who spank."[81] One Saturday evening in May, Galloway closes his store and goes to spend the evening, as he always does, at the home of his friend Musak. "Would he have spent that evening differently, or would he have tried to enjoy it more, if he had foreseen that it was his last evening as a happy man? To this question and many others, including that of whether he had ever been really happy, he would later have to try to find an answer."[82]

Notes of foreboding like the above, similar warnings of impending tragedy, occur at the beginning of many of Simenon's novels. Richter explains that the reason for such warnings is that the protagonist is inadequate for the tragic role he must play. The seriousness of destiny does not correspond to the insignificance of the individual whom it destroys. Thus, Simenon's hero is at a loss when tragedy strikes. He is on unfamilar ground and doesn't know what to do. He is disoriented by tragedy because he is unable to recognize it when it appears and it is his blindness as he stumbles into misfortune that these first pages describe.[83]

When Galloway leaves his friend and returns home at midnight, he discovers that his son, Ben, has run off with a fifteen year old girl, abandoning him just as his wife did years before when Ben was an infant. Since then, Galloway's only thought has been for his son's happiness. Now, he realizes that his belief in the close relationship between them had been an illusion, since his son had kept such a major decision from him. His anguish grows as he learns that Ben has robbed and killed a man, and his first reaction is an instinctive desire to protect his son. "Never had he felt so sharply, so physically, the bond that existed between them. It was not a separate person who was in trouble somewhere, God knew where—it was a part of himself."[84] Because he fears that Ben may be shot down by the police, he agrees to tape a radio message asking the boy to give himself up, sobbing that he will always be on his side no matter what happens. He knows that people will be almost certain to think that he is sending his radio appeal to put himself on the right side of the law, but this is not true. "He was not trying to show himself in a favorable light, or to evade his responsibilities. Ben was himself; he was ready to stand judgment in his stead and to accept the punishment."[85]

When Ben refuses to see his father after he is arrested, the inspector tells Galloway sympathetically that parents, without exception, are the last to know their own children. When he does see his son, Galloway understands what the policeman had been trying to tell him. "It was as though sixteen years of shared life and daily intimacy had suddenly ceased to exist. There had been no glint in his son's eyes, no emotion on his face. Nothing but a knitting of his brows, as when one sees something unpleasant in one's way."[86]

Ben is sentenced to life imprisonment, and Dave returns to his home, where he attempts to understand why his apparently ordinary son became a thief and a murderer. He has a frame made for three pictures, one of his father at thirty-eight, of himself at twenty-two, and of Ben at sixteen. "It seemed to him that those three photographs contained the explanation of everything that had happened, but he realized that he, alone, could understand. . . . Didn't the gaze of the three men reveal a shared secret life, a life, rather, that had been made to recoil upon itself? A look of timidity, almost a look of resignation, while the identical drawing in of the lips hinted at suppressed revolt. Some people are able to prevent their revolt from coming to the surface for their entire life, but with others it breaks out."[87] Only once in their lives, each one of the three had revolted. Galloway's father, who had bowed his head all his life, had once stayed out all night—an act that might pass for revolt—and had been made to pay for it by his wife every day of his life. His own revolt had been to marry the town tramp, while Ben, at sixteen, had carried his revolt to an extreme. All three had imagined that they were going to set themselves free, and each had had to pay for his act.

When Galloway discovers that Ben is to be a father, he hopes that his grandson will be free of the Galloway inferiority complex. "Often, in his apartment, in his shop, and even in the street, Dave talked in a low voice to his father and to his son, who went with him everywhere. Soon, he would talk to his grandson as well, to reveal to him the secret in men."[88] Simenon does not specify what this secret is. Claude Mauriac feels that it is the primacy of heredity because of the unbreakable links it forges,[89] while for Régis Boyer this secret is that men are terribly alone, terribly wicked, but terribly pitiful because they are unhappy, and it is better to try to understand and to love them than to judge them.[90] However, all such secrets in Simenon's work cannot be communicated, and it is because of the impossibility of communication that his heroes are alienated and condemned to solitude.

CHAPTER 4

Solitude and Alienation

I *Inability to Communicate*

SIMENON'S characters, immured in their solitude, exemplify his belief that basic human truths cannot be communicated. His characters are particularly incapable of communication because they are creatures of instinct rather than of intelligence. Fallois suggests that analysis would permit them to organize and formulate their ideas. Instead, they are dominated by vague ideas. "Assailed by images, they never stop thinking, but they never think in the strict sense of the word and we are party to the impressions that beset their consciousness as they try to wrench themselves free from them, as if from a trap."[1]

Such images had been preying on Mahé's mind for four years *(Le Cercle des Mahé)* and "he had not yet created a stir, he was satisfied to ruminate over a vague idea that was not yet a plan. He knew that one morning upon awakening he would be faced with a fixed idea, an idea completely in focus, and then woe unto those who tried to dissuade him from it."[2] Significantly, it was only when it was too late, when he was drowning, that Mahé "began to see the truth. . . . But when he finally reached this truth, when he blended with it like an air bubble, his life as a man had ended and he could no longer transmit his message."[3] Like Mahé, Simenon's other characters are unable to formulate their ideas lucidly. The truths they feel, expressed by the frequently used phrase "he knew what he meant," remain locked within them.

II *Sensuality as an Escape from Solitude*

The title *Les Complices*, suggesting a certain communion, is ironic, for it serves to bring into relief the desperate solitude of Joseph Lambert. The opening words, "It was brutal, instantaneous,"[4] set the mood for the remainder of the work. "And yet he was neither surprised nor resentful," the novel continues,

as if he had always been expecting it. He realized in a flash, as soon as the horn started behind him, that the catastrophe was inevitable and that it was his fault. It was not an ordinary horn that was pursuing him with a kind of anger and terror, but a mournful, agonizing howl such as one hears in a port on a foggy night. At the same time, he saw in his mirror the red and black bulk of a huge bus bearing down on him and the contracted face of a man with grizzled hair, and he realized that he himself was driving in the middle of the road. It did not occur to him to free his hand which Edmonde continued to press between her thighs. He would not have had time.[5]

The bus swerves on the wet pavement to avoid Lambert's car, leaves the road, crashes into a wall, and bursts into flames, killing the driver, two counselors, and forty-eight children on their way back to Paris from a summer camp. Lambert flees the holocaust almost instinctively. He thinks of stopping, but he cannot do so, he is driven forward by uncontrollable panic. He understands that he is assured the silent complicity of Edmonde. His wordless sexual encounters with her permit him a momentary escape from ordinary life into "a universe where all that matters is the quivering of his senses."[6] These brief moments also underline the fact that after a year of the most intimate relationship possible between a man and a woman, he still has no idea of what is going on in her head. Failing to find a response other than the fleeting one of her body, Lambert locks himself in his office and writes the words, "I am not guilty."[7] He understands, however, that these words will be misunderstood and, since he knows no others to explain that he is an innocent victim of destiny, he crumples the sheet and throws it into the wastebasket before shooting himself.

A desperate attempt to escape solitude through eroticism is evident in many of Simenon's novels. Charles Alavoine, in *Lettre à mon juge*, describes this frantic effort to lose oneself in another. "The more she belonged to me, the more I felt her to be mine, the more I judged her worthy of being mine . . . the more I felt the need to consume her even more. To consume her as I, for my part, would have wanted to merge completely with her."[8]

In his letter, Alavoine reveals the details of his life and the inexorable forces that led him to murder the only woman he ever loved. He was a successful doctor in the Vendée whose life was dominated

and controlled by his mother and wife. It had never occurred to him
to question whether or not he was happy. Nor had he realized
before that he was capable of passionate love. One night, on his way
back from the hospital of a neighboring city, he meets a young
woman at the station. They spend the night together, and Alavoine
realizes that this is the only time he has ever felt such passion.

Alavoine then introduces Martine into his home. "Did I even
know where we were going? There was only one thing I knew, it
was that I could no longer do without her and that I felt physical
pain as violent as that felt by the sickest of my patients as soon as
she was no longer near me, as soon as I did not see her, as soon as I
did not hear her."[9] When the situation at home becomes unbearable, Alavoine leaves his mother, wife, and children and goes to
live in Paris with Martine so that he may be with her continually.
"If you were to ask me how one recognizes love, if I had to diagnose
love, I would say: 'First the need for a presence . . . a need as
necessary, as absolute and as vital as a physical need.' "[10]

In Paris he has the exhilarating sensation of starting life anew,
but Martine's sordid past refuses to be buried. When he first met
Martine, she was desperate because she realized how low she had
sunk. She was filled with such self-hatred that she even con-
templated entering a brothel, for "there exists a degree of self-
disgust where one defiles oneself in order to touch bottom faster
because then nothing worse can happen."[11] Alavoine's love had
saved her from that fate and that was why she accepted his beatings
when he became tortured by jealousy of her former lovers. He
believed that there were two women inhabiting Martine's body, one
soiled by her past and the other the childishly pure one he had
restored by his love. Yet, despite herself, despite her love, Martine
could not rid herself of the other, "she was the other and she knew
it."[12] Alavoine finally kills Martine to exorcise the part of her that
was standing between them. "I had to kill the other once and for all
so that my Martine could live at last. I killed the other, fully conscious of what I was doing. . . . I killed her so that she might
live, and our eyes continue to embrace to the very end."[13]
Alavoine's final words, penned just before he kills himself to rejoin
his love, are: "We have gone as far as possible. We have done
everything possible. We wanted the totality of love."[14]

En cas de malheur is based on the same situation as *Lettre à mon
juge*. Here, too, a successful man, with an authoritarian, protective
wife, feels the need to explain the reasons for his sensual bondage to

a young slut. Maître Gobillet, Parisian criminal lawyer, first meets Yvette when she comes to his office to seek his help in defending her against a holdup charge. The saying in Paris goes that "if you're innocent, take any good lawyer. If you're guilty, get in touch with Maître Gobillet."[15] Yvette is guilty.

While Gobillet has always been unscrupulous in his methods, he goes to even greater extremes than usual to win this case. Following Yvette's acquittal, Gobillet becomes hopelessly caught by her animal nature. Analyzing her magnetic appeal, he remarks:

I've often slept with girls, both professionals and nonprofessionals and, when I think about it, I realize that they had certain things in common with Yvette. . . . My strongest impulse was probably a craving for pure sex . . . without any considerations of emotion or passion. Let's say sex in its raw state, the need to behave like an animal. I can't be with Yvette for an hour without feeling an urge to see her naked body, to touch her, to ask her to caress me. . . . Yvette . . . personifies for me the female, with her weaknesses, her cowardice, and also with her instinct to cling to the male and make herself his slave.[16]

Like Alavoine, Gobillet writes: "I cannot get along without her. . . . I suffer physically when I am away from her."[17] Gobillet's frenzied sensuality is prompted by a desire to lose himself in "another world in which certain preoccupations disappear, where the importance of things changes."[18] He is seized with a "certain nostalgia for a different life, for a life that would be like that described in the speeches at prize-giving ceremonies and in picture books."[19]

III   *Alcohol as an Escape from Solitude*

In other novels, it is alcohol rather than sensuality that permits the characters to break loose from their everyday lives and breathe at a higher level. Not many drinks are required for Steve *(Feux rouges)* to go "into the tunnel. . . . He knew exactly what it meant and what it was like to be in the tunnel; yet, curiously, when he was there he never allowed himself to admit the fact, except for occasional brief instants, and always too late."[20] Steve Hogan is a confused, resentful man, who thinks he can hold his liquor. He is jealous of his efficient, pretty wife whose income is equal to his and who arranges their life in her own way. Steve has two children at summer camp in Maine, a Madison Avenue job, and a mortgaged

house in the suburbs, all of which contribute to his feeling of en-
trapment. He gets the chance to "get a little outside of everyday
life"[21] when he and his wife take an automobile trip to Maine to
pick up their children. Steve starts drinking even before they leave.
When he continues, his wife leaves him to go on by bus. In the
course of his drunken wandering from one bar to another, Steve
picks up Sid Halligan, an escaped convict, who he confusedly feels
symbolizes the fulfillment of his own rebellion against convention.
He unburdens himself to Sid in a drunken monologue: "They
create rules that they call laws, and they call sin everything that
frightens them in others. That's the truth, old boy! If they didn't
tremble, if they were real men, they wouldn't need policemen and
courts, ministers and churches."[22]

The next morning, Steve reads in the newspaper that his wife was
robbed and raped on the highway by Sid Halligan before Steve ran
into him. Steve's physical sobering up is accompanied by a spiritual
sobering up as he begins to understand that he had a drunkard's
determination to soil everything and that the man in whom he con-
fided was an incorrigible criminal. "Now he had seen the end of the
road. He could look elsewhere, return to everyday life; he looked
about him, surprised to find them all so tense and said in his normal
voice: 'That's all.' "[23]

Alcohol is the means by which Antoine (*Antoine et Julie*)
desperately attempts to flee the loneliness and boredom of his existence. What he seeks when he drinks is "that contact, that way of
looking at humanity and of feeling at one with it."[24] At times, Antoine would stretch out his hand to touch a table or a wall, "to
assure himself of their stability, but that wouldn't reassure him
about himself. If the world really existed, he still had to find out
what he was doing in it and what those people around him were doing who put so much seriousness, so much feeling, into their actions."[25] Antoine is never at peace with himself. When drinking, he
can achieve an illusion of peace, but the rest of the time he realizes
that "a man is worth nothing at all. What counts is to put on an
act. . . . As for him, what difference would it make, since inside it
would always be the same thing. The same thing: that is,
nothing."[26]

Antoine's increasing dependence on alcohol precipitates the
tragic conclusion to an already floundering marriage. The climactic
scene occurs when Antoine and Julie go to a restaurant to celebrate
Christmas Eve. He goes out to get her gift from the cloakroom,

takes a drink on the way, and leaves her sitting in the restaurant to go off on a drunken binge. When he telephones their apartment the next day, a nurse answers and tells him that Julie has had another heart attack. Thenceforth, the tone of their relationship changes. They have come to a tacit understanding, and Julie realizes that she must never ask him to come home early, that she must avoid certain words and certain frightened or resigned attitudes. "They would speak gently without hatred or bitterness, in voices that lacked resonance."[27] Antoine concentrates on doing the same things every day, dispassionately, without believing in them. When the effect of one drink wears off, he takes another which automatically puts him back into the desired state. He decides quite calmly that he knows why so many people don't commit suicide: "There comes a moment, if you know how to manage things, when it is no longer necessary."[28]

One night, Antoine goes out to buy Julie's medicine. Instead of going home with it, he stays out drinking. When he finally does arrive, Julie is dead. Thereafter, he lives alone; nothing is touched in the house and no one passes through the doors. He stops drinking and every day, whatever the weather, he goes to the cemetery, where the headstone contains a blank space for his name alongside of Julie's.

Antoine's devotion to his dead wife raises questions about the failure of their marriage. They really love one another with a tender love devoid of "romantic illusions."[29] Unfortunately, with the best intentions in the world, they act upon one another with disastrous effect. Each one would like to make the other happy and, instead, causes only suffering. "Why couldn't we become an exception?"[30] Antoine would think. But then he would furnish the answer himself. "Why should they be exceptions? Why shouldn't the thousands of men and women who walk up and down the Champs-Elysées have the same sort of problems?"[31]

IV *The Failure of the Couple*

That Simenon's characters rarely succeed in linking their lives to another is, he maintains, a faithful reflection of reality, adding: "What people call 'love' varies in each individual. All my characters have known one type of love or another. . . . For most of the individuals I know, love plays the same role I assign it in my novels . . . there are very few whose lives are given over entirely to love, and there aren't many either for whom love is a beautiful thing."[32]

Simenon's work contains endless variations on the theme of the failure of a couple to achieve true union, from the sexual bondage of Alavoine and Gobillet, through the misalliance of Antoine and Julie, the hatred of the elderly couple in *Le Chat*, to the detestation leading to murder in *L'Escalier de fer* and *Dimanche*. A recurring image symbolizing this failure is that of the suddenly empty home. The husband returns one day to find that his wife has abandoned him. It happens to Dave Galloway in Connecticut and to Jonas Milk in the Berry, to M. Monde *(La Fuite de M. Monde)*, Loursat *(Les Inconnus dans la maison)*, and to Cardinaud *(Le Fils Cardinaud)*. At first, all of them are bewildered by a seemingly inexplicable abandonment but, as they begin to reflect, they understand that it was the culmination of a long misunderstanding that only their blindness had hidden from them.

The protagonist of *Les Innocents*, one of the innocents of the title, is at peace with himself and with the world, principally because he has always accepted people and things at their face value, never seeking to penetrate beneath the surface. When the novel begins, Célerin is at work, enveloped in the warmth and well-being of his workshop. Suddenly, the quiet is interrupted by the arrival of a policeman, who announces that Célerin's wife has just been run over by a bus. As Célerin reflects on his life, after the funeral, he realizes that he lived with his wife for twenty years without ever having known her. Although he had always revealed his most intimate thoughts to her, she never spoke about herself, for, in truth, he had never been more than a stranger to her, a stranger who shared her bed. In a final effort to comprehend the essence of their relationship, Célerin goes to the site of the accident. There he makes the shattering discovery that for eighteen of the twenty years of his marriage, during which he had been the happiest man in the world, his wife had been his best friend's mistress.

Like Célerin, Jeantet *(Le Veuf)* had no more of a premonition of his wife's abandonment "than travelers on a train who eat in the dining car, read, talk, doze, or watch the countryside go by a few instants before the catastrophe."[33] He discovers only after his wife commits suicide that his marriage had been a disaster, that he had stifled her with his so-called goodness. He had married a prostitute because it was "necessary for him that she be guilty, ashamed, and miserable because he could not have endured to live with a normal wife."[34] Jeantet belongs to the vast fraternity of men in Simenon's work who cannot be part of a successful couple because they are insecure in their masculinity. Filled with doubt and self-hatred, they are able to relate only to soiled women to whom they can feel superior. Like Jeantet, the protagonist of *Le Temps d'Anaïs* is impotent except with prostitutes and his wife, one of a long series of nymphomaniacs in Simenon's cast of characters. He had never considered himself to be a real man sexually and tells the psychiatrist that he was pleased that his wife was what she was and that she degraded herself by sleeping with anyone. His contempt for her lessened to a certain extent the contempt he felt for himself.

In general, there is no open confrontation between husband and wife in Simenon's novels. Marriages break apart soundlessly, as husbands and wives sink into mutually ill-tempered daily existence. At times, however, the silent struggle leads to murderous consequences. *Dimanche* opens on the Sunday that Emile has selected to murder his wife, Berthe, an act he has been preparing for eleven months. "As he looked back, it seemed short. He was surprised to have suddenly arrived so near to the end, and, though he still had no temptation to shrink back, he was nonetheless seized with a certain giddiness."[35] Through flashbacks, Simenon then explains the circumstances that have led Emile, an ordinary man, to this desperate act. Emile is the chef in a small hotel on the Côte d'Azur that belongs to his wife. Her marrying him was the first in a long series of humiliations to which she subjected him. She had bought him "more safely and surely than by any contract duly signed and sealed."[36] Emile involves himself in an affair with a half-wild servant girl whom he compares to a happy animal. "Wasn't it rather in the manner of an animal that she loved him? Nothing else counted for her but to live in his wake, and the moment he made a sign to her, she would come running to bury herself in his arms. She was at once his pet dog and his slave. She did not judge him, did not try to understand him or guess what he was thinking. She had adopted him as a master, just as a stray dog, for no apparent reason, attaches itself to the heels of a passer-by."[37]

Because he is insecure in his virility, Emile is able to relate only to this "slave." When his wife discovers his liaison, she subjects him to constant humiliation until he decides he must kill her. "It is claimed that a man can live a long time without eating or drinking. It is more difficult to live without one's pride, and his wife had taken it away."[38] Many of the murders in Simenon's work are motivated by wounded pride. Donald Dodd *(La Main)* finally kills the perfect wife whose self-righteousness has humiliated him throughout their marriage. "I understood the look my wife gave me. As always, there was no reproach. Not even a silent warning. It was a special kind of look, and I had seen it over and over again through the years, probably since we had known each other. In that look lay a whole catalogue of indictments. . . . Was I afraid of that look of hers? Just as, when I was a child, I had been afraid to meet my mother's eyes."[39]

While Dodd acts spontaneously when pushed beyond endurance, Emile meticulously plans his actions and waits for the propitious moment to enact the perfect crime. An even more cunning counteraction on his wife's part provides the surprise ending that is unusual in Simenon's work. Berthe, with the intuition of a mother who anticipates her child's misbehavior, has understood that Emile has poisoned her lunch. When he finally goes out to the terrace to see what is happening, he sees his mistress eating it instead. Berthe is standing over her and, with a look, tells him that he had better not intervene. "He sought for a plausible reason to leave as soon as all the customers had been served. He could find none. He lacked lucidity. Then, there was Berthe standing in the doorway. . . . 'You haven't forgotten the football match?' Berthe was saying in a natural voice. . . . Berthe was right. It was high time to leave for Cannes and to mingle with the crown attending the football match. She would see to everything. It was better that way. When he came back, it would be all over."[40]

Murder is also the way in which Etienne Lomel's wife (L'Escalier de fer) intends to rid herself of him in order to marry her young lover. As Lomel, with resignation, makes daily note of the progress of his poisoning by his wife, he feels a terrible need for protection, affection, and human warmth. He now understands the reason for the death of her first husband and that, when he was her lover, he had signed the man's death warrant by answering yes when she asked whether he would marry her if she were free. That is why he is not outraged when he realizes that the situation is being repeated. He had always known that something terrible would happen sooner or later and it was, he felt, no more than he deserved because he had kept silent the other time and, therefore, was as guilty as she. That was why he had felt the need through the years to lose himself in his wife, to become one with her, because it was for this that the murder had been committed; and it was their only excuse, if any excuse were admissible. When Etienne discovers the identity of Louise's lover, he feels neither anger nor a desire for vengeance, but decides that he must kill him in order to regain Louise's love. He finally confronts the young man, but turns the gun on himself instead, aware that Louise will always be denied him and that he must pay for his tacit consent to her first murder.

Louise's motivation is more clearly comprehensible than that of Bébé Donge who, one Sunday, tries to poison her husband because he has not been able to recognize the exceptional nature of her love for him. While Bébé is being held for trial, her husband, François, realizes that he had been wrong in marrying a young girl, "bringing her into a house and then abandoning her to her solitude. Not even her own solitude! Solitude in an alien atmosphere which can seem hostile!"[41] He understands how absurd it had been to offend one another for ten years, to waste the ten best years of their lives hurting one another, living side by side without mutual understanding. François wonders whether he had been a monster not to have seen all that before or whether it was only because he was an ordinary, fallible man. While he had misunderstood her to the point of hating her, "she had loved him to the point of total despair. And he had noticed nothing."[42] When Bébé leaves at the end of the trial to serve her five year term, François is no longer the same man. He has decided to wait for her to see whether married love can indeed be a spiritual meeting of souls, although Bébé has told him it is too late, that she had waited and hoped for too long.

V *A Few Couples Succeed*

Successful relationships between men and women stand out in Simenon's work because of their rarity. Maigret's happiness is dependent on the fact that his wife is satisfied to assume a passive role, acting rather like a servant or a paid companion. Her life is one of service and dedication to Maigret. Another successful marriage is that of Omer and Maria Petermans (*Le Clan des Ostendais*), which is more of an equal partnership since Omer respects his wife's opinions and consults her before making any decisions, even in matters relating to his profession. Also, counterbalancing Etienne and his murderous wife in *L'Escalier de fer* are their friends Arthur and Mariette Leduc, patterned on Simenon's uncle Léopold and his wife, Eugénie, the canteen girl.

Leduc, the son of a wealthy attorney, had come to Paris to study law, but left his studies to become a *chansonnier*. He and Mariette, a fishmonger's daughter whom he would eventually marry, led a hand-to-mouth existence while he tried newspaper publicity, painting, and selling. After a series of jobs, none of which lasted very long, he contented himself with spending his days in various Montmartre cafés, while his wife, who loved him as he was, supported him with the proceeds of her millinery shop.

The Leducs, who play a secondary role in *L'Escalier de fer*, prefigure Bob and Lulu, the protagonists of *Le Grand Bob*. Like Arthur, Bob had many jobs because he was never able to settle down and take life seriously. His favorite expression, "crevant" (hysterically funny), repeated at every opportunity, expressed his opinion of life and its responsibilities. His good humor and gaiety were contagious; he had only to approach people for their faces to light up. Lulu, like Mariette, adores her husband, whom she also supports by running a hat shop. In their apartment behind the shop, Bob and Lulu receive their many friends at all hours of the day and night.

Bob and Lulu's story is told by their friend, a Parisian doctor named Charles Coindreau, who had met them at a fisherman's inn at Tilly on the Seine where they spent their weekends. One Monday, Charles receives a call from Lulu informing him that Bob drowned the day before at Tilly. As Coindreau makes inquiries into the drowning, he discovers that it was not accidental, but a carefully planned suicide. "Having decided to kill himself, he was concerned to do so decently. It was in character. He had run through all the forms of suicide, searching for the one that would look most like an accident."[43] At Tilly, there were two groups of guests: the fishermen who went to bed early and rose at 4:30 to indulge in their passion, and the night people who stayed up drinking, dancing, and playing cards. Bob and Lulu belonged to the second group. The efforts of the fishermen were incomprehensible to Bob, whose favorite witticism was: "Man is not made for work. The proof of this is that it makes him tired."[44] That was why his decision to join the anglers two weeks before his death met with such great astonishment on the part of the other habitués of the inn. When his body is found on the second Sunday, it is assumed that his death was accidental until the discovery is made that the line was wrapped around his ankle twice, an occurrence that had to be deliberate. Why, Lulu asks Charles, "you who knew him well, why would he have done that? . . . Do you think it's because of me? . . . And I, all my life, thought I was making him happy!"[45]

As Charles makes his inquiries into Bob's life and death, the story develops on three levels. The mystery surrounding Bob's suicide, the least interesting of the three, is solved by the discovery that he had stomach cancer. "He did not kill himself because he was afraid of suffering, but because he didn't want to afflict others with the sight of his suffering and with what he considered to be a downfall."[46] On another level, the novel touches upon one of the central themes in Simenon's work, that of a middle-aged man who is prompted by an unexpected event to reassess all that he had previously taken for granted. When Charles reviews the completely honest relationship that existed between Bob and Lulu, he realizes the limitations in his own marriage. He is tempted to tell his wife the truth about his feelings for her and about their marriage, but he decides that it is too late in their relationship for such honesty. Bob was honest with Lulu from the start. "When Bob adopted Lulu, he accepted complete responsibility for her. He never made great speeches to her. He never even spoke to her of love. The long and short of it is that he took her by the hand like a child, like the small girl that she was, and she, surprised at first that a great boy like him should bend down to her level, had confidence in him and, consequently, confidence in life."[47] Charles begins to understand that the carefree atmosphere of Bob and Lulu's home resulted from their honesty and their ability to recognize what was important in life and worthy of their attention.

The most fascinating aspect of the novel is an examination of the character of Bob. As Charles continues his investigation, he discovers that Bob was the son of the dean of the University of Poitiers. When he was seventeen years old, his ambition had been to become an army priest in the Sahara desert. Then, one day, he decided that he would never make either a good priest or a good officer and that, deep down, he lacked religious faith. After he passed his baccalaureate, he entered law school and spent one of his vacations as an unskilled worker on the night shift in the Citroen plant with impoverished foreign workers. When Coindreau reflects on Bob's background, he decides that Bob had first aimed too high, and then too low, and had finally settled into joyful mediocrity.[48]

By all conventional standards, Bob was a failure, for, despite his background and education, he spent his life in the bistros of Montmartre supported by a wife whom he had virtually pulled out of the gutter. But he was a happy man because he led the life he had chosen. One day, when his sister asked him whether he was happy, he told her that he would not have changed his life for any other. "Having wished to be a saint in the desert, then the most humble of the humble, he had finished, quite simply, as he told her, by devoting himself to making one person happy."[49] Bob had also remarked that if everyone would take it upon himself to ensure the happiness of another person, the whole world would be happy.[50]

Lulu, like Simenon's Aunt Eugénie, can find no reason to live without her love. She tells Coindreau that she has the same dream every night, in which she doesn't see Bob clearly, but only a shadowy form. Only the arm seems to be alive and it beckons her to join him. Then she seems to hear a moan and she tells herself that he is complaining because she is staying behind too long.[51] Two weeks before Christmas, Lulu kills herself rather than spend it without Bob. On the bed next to her body lie a crumpled photograph of her and Bob taken fifteen years previously and an empty vial of sleeping pills. If she had held on a few weeks longer, she would have needed no drugs, for she "weighed no more than a ten year old child."[52]

Trois chambres à Manhattan, written three months after *Lettre à mon juge*, brings a similar situation to a happy ending. For the first time in Simenon's work, a man and a woman find communion and happiness together. Simenon had just met and fallen in love with Denise Ouimet, who was to become his second wife, and the novel reflects an optimistic outlook on love. Simenon states that the book coincided with a turning in his own life, the start of a new existence on a new continent and the founding of a new family. "You may perhaps have noticed," he continued,

that from the time of *Trois chambres à Manhattan* onward, my female characters have become less two dimensional, less hard and less ruthless than before. . . . I have the impression that at the age of forty . . . I was suddenly seized with a wish to understand women; till then I had only wanted to make use of them, in my novels, I mean. I made use of them as companions for the male character and to round off a story, but basically I suppose that, up to that time, I had known only one kind of woman. Suddenly, I discovered that there were other kinds.[53]

François Combe, the protagonist of *Trois chambres à Manhattan*, unlike Alavoine, succeeds in wiping out the past and accepting love with all of its compromises. His love also results from a chance meeting with a lonely, world-weary woman, which is followed by an aimless, rambling nocturnal walk through deserted streets, culminating at dawn in passionate coupling in a small hotel room. When Kay confesses to Combe that she was at the end of her endurance when she met him and had decided to follow the first man who came along, Combe judges her with cold lucidity: "She's the three o'clock in the morning type of woman, the one who cannot make up her mind to go to bed, who needs to keep up her state of excitement, to drink, to smoke, to speak, to finally fall into a man's arms when her nerves are frayed out."[54] But then he becomes aware that Kay is indispensable to him and he is resigned to stop struggling against his love no matter what he may learn about her past. He understands that the past does not matter, since they are starting afresh. "To begin a life from scratch. Two lives. Two lives from scratch."[55] Combe expects not only a definitive obliteration of the past by their love, but also a passport to a new life. It seems to him that he has gone full circle to arrive there. When he goes out into the street "all that he sees about him, this pilgrimage into a world of grey shadows, in which dark men move agitatedly in the beams of the electric lights, those stores, those movie theaters with their wreaths of lights, those stands selling sickening hot dogs or pastry, those penny arcades, those jukeboxes, everything a big city has been able to invent to beguile solitude, he can finally look at all that henceforth without panic or disgust."[56]

François, like Simenon's other characters, is unable to express his feelings. It is enough for him and Kay to look at one another for him to have an almost "sacrilegious feeling of being present at the birth of happiness."[57] They do not embrace, but stand quietly cheek to cheek for a long time. They know that they will never be alone again and when Kay suddenly shudders and Combe feels at almost the same time an old forgotten anguish rise in his throat, they understand that they have both thrown a last glance at their former solitude. "And both wonder how they were able to bear it."[58]

The novel ends when their life together begins, as does *Le Voyageur de la Toussaint*, in which the protagonist flees an unhappy marriage for a woman whose conception of life coincides with his. In *Le Voyageur de la Toussaint*, Gilles Mauvoisin, a young man of twenty, the son of itinerant music hall performers, arrives secretly in the city of La Rochelle from which his parents had run off to elope many years before. Gilles's parents have just died accidentally during a tour of Norway and Gilles has only their native city and the relatives they left behind to fall back on. He discovers that he is heir to the fortune of his uncle who had been one of the wealthiest and most detested citizens of the city. He also discovers that his uncle

left him the key to a vault in which he had accumulated compromising documents on all of the prominent citizens of La
Rochelle, documents that had permitted him to maintain control
over them. Now that he is dead, they are anxious to destroy the
papers.

The novel has the makings of a first rate detective story as Gilles
sets out to discover which one of the many people who detested his
uncle had finally poisoned him. His inquiries plunge him into a
mass of intrigue in which he finds himself surrounded by the hostility of the small group of politicians, bankers, and businessmen who
control the economy of the city. Nevertheless, motivated by a sense
of duty, he continues the struggle. He marries and has a child and
lives in a manner in keeping with his vast wealth. He also destroys
the compromising documents. No longer fearing his uncle's
revelations, the people are able to do what they had always wanted
to do, forget. They are simple people, occupied with petty interests;
capable of a great deal of hypocrisy and cruelty when the values
they place above all else—money and respectibility—are threatened, but desirous above all to live in peace.[59]

The citizens of La Rochelle believe that Gilles has become one of
them because he sits in an office, makes telephone calls, writes
columns of figures, concerns himself with cars and trucks, writes up
bills, signs checks and bills of exchange, and greets people distractedly in the street.[60] They do not understand that he, like his
parents, is the wandering type and that he must leave once his job
has been done. Gilles has fallen in love with his uncle's widow,
Colette; because she is of the same race as he, only she is able to understand that he is being stifled by his inheritance. Gilles and
Colette leave together at the end of the novel to take up in their
turn the life of his parents. Gilles abandons his wife, child, and fortune, because he believes that Colette represents his only chance for
happiness.

This novel provides an excellent illustration of the unconventional sense of morality possessed by Simenon's heroes, for whom
morality is not an absolute dictated by the intelligence and the will,
but an individual choice. Judged by conventional moral standards,
Gilles is wrong to abandon his wife and child, but Simenon has
always been detached from conventional morality. True morality
for him is very personal and resembles love of sacrifice; it is the
response to a call. Gilles abandons a wife and child who do not need
him to rescue Colette from solitude and despair.

CHAPTER 5

Flight

I *Novels of Flight*

THE principal theme in the work of Georges Simenon is escape, both physical and psychological. In a group of novels, Simenon deals with middle-aged men who, after years of conforming to the standards of society, flee their milieu. Jacques Dubois has traced the pattern common to all of the novels that deal with this theme. A certain event causes the hero to break with his habits, his duties, and the type of life he has led; his break is often consummated by a crime; his evasion brings him adventure and initiates him into a certain seedy side of life; although his liberation is consecrated by a redemption, he fails—either he goes mad or comes back to his point of departure with a knowledge of the meaninglessness of existence; but the hero who has the courage to take the measure of his life and then return has acquired a form of second sight that helps him to survive.[1]

II *Mechanical Routine of Daily Life*

Before their awakening, the lives of all of these men are characterized by mechanical repetition of a series of gestures and actions, almost as if ritual exorcised the misfortune that might otherwise overtake them. Dave Galloway, the watchmaker of Everton, "followed the routine of every evening, or more exactly of Saturdays, which were a little different from other days. . . . He no longer noticed that every day he went through the same motions, in the same order, and that it was this, perhaps, that gave him so peaceful and reassuring an aspect."[2] Steve Adams, in *Le Passage de la ligne*, describes his father as belonging "to that train compartment that carried to London, every day at the same time, people belonging to the same class as he, with similar professions, who were leaving behind them more or less similar houses and families. Each morning on the way in, each evening on the way back, they greeted one another with a gesture as restrained as a masonic greeting."[3] For fifteen years, Doctor Hans Kupérus of Sneek *(L'Assassin)* "insisted that the same gestures be performed at the same times and that all the rites of a well-organized life be observed."[4] The first few pages of *Le Bourgemestre de Furnes* trace in half minute segments Terlinck's occupations at the end of the business day. As *Le Bilan Malétras* opens, Malétras mechanically pulls his cigar case out of his pocket, repeating the same scene that has been taking place at the same time for years. Sticking out his chest, Malétras fingers his vest, takes a gold cigar-cutter in the form of a guillotine out of his right vest pocket, and extracts an expensive gold lighter from another pocket. After lighting his cigar, he replaces the articles in his pockets, emits a deep sigh, leans back a little in his chair, and watches the smoke rise with half-closed eyes. M. Monde *(La Fuite de Monsieur Monde)*, Bergelon *(Bergelon)*, Loursat *(Les Inconnus dans la maison)*, and Charles *(Oncle Charles s'est enfermé)* have similarly established routines that permit them to live automatically, thereby obviating the need either to appraise the meaning of their lives or to make an existential choice.

III   *Break with Routine*

The break, or crisis, seems at times to occur spontaneously, but this is only because the cause is not readily apparent. In such cases, however, it is the culmination of a situation that has been developing subliminally for a long time. Alavoine *(Lettre à mon juge)* does not recognize this slow maturation when he writes:

There was just a moment when I began to look around me with different eyes and I saw a city that seemed foreign to me, a pretty city, very light, very clean, very bright, a city in which everyone greeted me with affability.
Why then did I have the feeling of emptiness?
I also began to look at my house and I wondered why it was my house, what relationship these rooms, this garden, this gate adorned with a copper name plate bearing my name had with me.
I looked at Armande and I had to remind myself that she was my wife.
Why?
And those two little girls who called me papa. . . . What was I doing there, in a small, peaceful city, in a pretty, comfortable house among people who smiled at me and who shook my hand familiarly?

And who had established that daily routine that I followed as scrupulously as if my life depended on it? What am I saying! As if, from the beginning of time, it had been decided by the Creator that that routine would inexorably be mine.[5]

More often, a specific event occurs that causes the protagonist to break with his habits and daily routine. Terlinck *(Le Bourgemestre de Furnes)* compares this awakening to a scene familiar to the citizens of Ostend: "They would bring a child who had never seen the ocean, whom they had blindfolded so that his first impression would be stronger. Once on the jetty, they abruptly removed the blindfold and the child would look at this infinitely vast horizon with anguish; he would quake at the knees, as if he were losing his footing, as if he felt himself being drawn into the abyss of the universe. Finally, panic-stricken, he would clutch hold of his father's legs, his mother's skirt, and burst into tears."[6]

Doctor Hans Kupérus's rupture is caused by an anonymous letter denouncing his wife as an adultress. Armed with this letter, he returns surreptitiously from his weekly professional trip to Amsterdam and kills his wife and her lover. Ostracized by the townspeople, who suspect him without being able to prove that he committed the crime, he begins to audit his life and discovers that he was jealous, not of his wife but of her lover. For fifteen years, Kupérus had followed the rules, but his wife's lover had lived without rules and he had succeeded in everything he undertook. This being the case, it was Kupérus who had been wrong and that was why he had to kill. Kupérus must pay the price for his discovery. He has gone too far in his quest for self-knowledge and what he has seen is terrifying. Unable to turn back from the brink, he escapes into madness.

IV   *Descent into Madness*

Like Kupérus, Popinga *(L'Homme qui regardait passer les trains)* murders and ultimately sinks into madness. He is a drab, little man who lives in a stable, well-ordered, logical universe where everything, including his wife, is of the finest quality. Kees, however, has dreamed of adventure. Night trains symbolized another life for him. "In them he sensed something strange, almost depraved. . . . It seemed to him that people who leave in that way leave forever."[7] Precisely because Kees has felt such yearning, he follows a rigid routine, fearful that nothing could stop him any longer were he to give way on a single point. In the evening, when the family sits near the ceramic stove, when his daughter starts to do her homework and his wife pastes pictures into an album while he turns the radio dial aimlessly, he is tempted to rise and shout out that family life is desperately boring.

One evening, Popinga meets his boss, Julius Coster, in a bar where he has been drinking heavily. He informs Popinga that he has embezzled vast sums of money and that, as a result, the firm is going bankrupt. Popinga will be losing not only his job but all his savings, which have been invested in the firm. Coster tells him that he is going to simulate suicide and then take off to join his mistress, Paméla, in Amsterdam. He destroys Popinga's final illusions when he reveals that Mrs. Coster, whom Popinga has always admired, is the mistress of the town doctor. Suddenly, Popinga recognizes a truth he has always suspected, that the orderly, logical world in which he lives is a collective lie, upheld by a universal, tacit agreement. He feels a desperate need to know what else life has to offer, to do everything that propriety had previously forbidden. At the age of forty, he decides to live as he pleases, without worrying about laws and customs, for he has discovered that no one else really takes them seriously.

Popinga takes the train to Amsterdam and goes to Paméla's hotel room. When she laughs in his face and humiliates him by refusing to grant him the favors she so freely bestows on everyone else, he strangles her. From Amsterdam, he takes the night train to Paris, because he thinks that there he will be able to realize all his stifled desires. In Paris, Popinga has a series of adventures with automobile thieves, prostitutes, and pimps, loses his money to a confidence man, wanders from one furnished room to another, attempts a second murder, and writes letters to the newspapers. "For forty years," he writes, "I looked at life like the poor little boy who presses his nose against the window of a pastry shop and watches others eat the pastries. Now I know that the pastries belong to those who bother to take them."[8] After an abortive attempt at suicide, he winds up in an insane asylum. There, he decides to write "the truth about the Kees Popinga case,"[9] in an effort to convince himself that his experiences were not without meaning. When the doctor asks him to produce the book in which he has been writing his memoirs, Popinga gives him only blank pages. The truth that Popinga has been unable to set down is that one cannot change one's life or live one's dreams.

This message, which is repeated throughout Simenon's work, has caused a critic to refer to him as the "novelist of useless flight."[10]

Both *L'Assassin* and *L'Homme qui regardait passer les trains* retain certain qualities of the detective novel including murder, suspense, and pursuit. The conclusion of both, the descent into madness, is the type of conclusion for which Simenon has been faulted. It has been suggested that, when it is time to end the novel, he often tacks on arbitrary, hasty conclusions.[11]

V *Return to Everyday Life*

Other novels dealing with the theme of flight have less melodramatic conclusions. *La Fuite de Monsieur Monde* is representative of this second group in which the hero returns at the end of the novel with a serenity stemming from an acceptance of his own humanity. M. Monde, Simenon's version of Everyman, is a successful businessman. He gets up every morning at the same time, goes to his office, and does his work there with the solemnity appropriate to the performance of a ritual. However, on the morning of his forty-eighth birthday, as he is walking to his office, he unaccountably raises his head, looks upward, and sees the chimneys of the buildings outlined against a pale blue sky in which a tiny, white cloud is floating. From that moment on, he changes. He feels ill at ease in his home and office and realizes that he must leave. "There was no inner debate . . . there was no decision to make, no decision at all."[12] Little by little, he changes his outer appearance to conform to the changes taking place within him. He shaves off his mustache, exchanges his finely tailored clothes for an ordinary, ill-fitting suit of the type worn by the man in the street. Then, almost automatically, he boards a bus for the Gare de Lyon. "He hadn't decided that he would do one thing or another. He was still following a program that had been drawn up in advance, but this time it hadn't been drawn up by him."[13] Just as automatically, he takes a train to Marseilles. When he arrives at the seashore, he begins to cry:

What streamed out from his being through his two eyes was all the fatigue accumulated for forty-eight years, and if those tears were sweet, it was because now the ordeal was over.

He had given up. He no longer struggled. He had hastened from far off—the train did not exist, but only an immense movement of flight—he had rushed toward the sea which, vast and blue, more alive than anyone, soul of the earth, soul of the world, breathed peacefully near him. . . . He spoke without opening his mouth because it wasn't necessary. He spoke of his infinite fatigue which stemmed not from the train trip but from his long journey as a man.[14]

Life seeks him out, however, as a young woman in the hotel room adjoining his attempts suicide because she has been abandoned by her lover. He rushes in and saves her life and they go off to Nice together. When the money he has brought with him is stolen, he has a feeling of relief, since the last vestige of his former life has disappeared with it. He and the young woman get jobs in a nightclub, she as hostess and he as kitchen supervisor. In his new life, he rediscovers the forgotten physical world of childhood. "He had become accustomed once again to the smell of his sweat, as he had when he was a child. For too many years, for the greater part of his life, he had forgotten the smell of sweat, the smell of the sun, all of life's smells that people no longer sniff because they are too busy with their affairs."[15]

One night, his first wife comes into the nightclub. She is a drug addict down on her luck. The sense of responsibility he feels toward her, although she had abandoned him soon after their marriage, makes him realize that one cannot discard one's past. He had always envied those who were carefree and footloose, and had become like them for a time. Now he knows that he must return to Paris and resume his former life. It seems to those about him that he has not changed. They do not understand his new serenity, the serenity of those who have decided to look squarely at themselves and at others, accepting their limitations and inadequacies, those who have "laid all ghosts and lost all shadows."[16] And he is unable to tell them about this change, for his discovery is one that must be made by each man himself, it is a truth that cannot be transmitted.

Like Monde, Malétras (*Le Bilan Malétras*) had planned his days minutely. "It wasn't a mania, it was a hygienic measure. He needed to lay out the days in that way, to divide them into blocks of time, he was convinced that it was thanks to that precaution that he maintained an unshakable equilibrum."[17] His equilibrium is destroyed when he strangles his young mistress in a fit of jealousy and finds that he has nothing to fall back on but self-awareness. As he takes the measure of his life, he realizes that he has lived for more than sixty years without wondering why he did one thing or another or where he was going or whether his actions had any meaning. Further probing reveals to him that nothing has meaning, that there is only one truth—"whatever a man does he is alone in life and in death"[18]—and that nothing is important but the "thread of his dream."[19] Like M. Monde, he intimidates those around him who are unable to understand a man "who is sufficient unto himself, coldly surveying others as a goldfish looks out at men through the sides of his bowl."[20]

While Loursat's flight *(Les Inconnus dans la maison)* had happened eighteen years before the opening of the novel when his wife had abandoned him and their infant daughter, he is forced in middle age to reevaluate his life. After his wife left, he cut himself off from the world and his legal profession and shut himself up in his study, drinking four bottles of wine daily and reading the contents of his vast library in a haphazard manner. His only contact with his daughter, Nicole, who has grown up without supervison, has been at mealtime. One night, Loursat hears a pistol shot and discovers a body in his attic. He realizes that he has become a stranger in his home and that he knows nothing about what has been taking place there. He discovers that Nicole is the leader of a band of rich adolescents who have been stealing for thrills and that their loot is stored in his attic. When he questions his daughter, he learns that the dead man is a criminal who had been blackmailing them. Since a culprit is needed by the police, Emile Manu, Nicole's lover and the only poor member of the band, is arrested. Loursat's sense of justice is outraged and he decides to undertake the defense of this young man who has been as humiliated by his poverty as Loursat was by his wife's departure. While the novel takes on the character of a detective novel as Loursat makes inquiries in order to discover the murderer, the real theme is the exploration of Loursat's character as he acquires insight into himself. "Why have I been living like a bear for eighteen years?" he wonders. "Because Geneviève had left him? Hadn't his life as a student in Paris been very similar to what it was now? Hadn't he, by the age of twenty, already learned to be by himself, with the poets and philosophers as his only companions? As the years had rolled on, things had become progressively thicker and murkier—that was all. . . . The truth was that Loursat had never tried to live. That's what struck him as he left home that evening."[21]

Armed with this insight, Loursat stops drinking to excess, unmasks the real culprit, and has Emile acquitted. The story of Loursat's return is one of Simenon's most affirmative conclusions. Not only does he return from his self-imposed exile, but he also assumes the role of redresser of grievances.

Charles Dupeux's exile within his own home *(Oncle Charles s'est enfermé)*, like that of Loursat, is triggered by a feeling of humiliation, but his lasts for only five days. It begins one day when he returns home carrying several packages. Instead of joining his wife and daughters at the dinner table, he goes up to the attic and locks himself in, refusing to answer their calls or explain his actions. Little by little, Simenon reveals who Charles is and why he has acted in this way. He is an ordinary man, husband, father, office worker, who is continually humiliated by his employer, who also happens to be his brother-in-law, Henri. One day Charles discovers Henri's secret. When Henri was young, he encouraged the debauchery of his wealthy associate, knowing that such excess would be fatal to someone with his fragile constitution. The proprietress of the brothel where he took the young man has been blackmailing him ever since.

Charles locks himself in the attic to think at leisure about what to do with Henri's secret and also with a windfall of 500,000 francs he has obtained at Henri's expense. Over the years, Charles stole small sums from the business. In addition, he misappropriated some shares of stock that suddenly shot up to 500,000 francs. Charles resolves the problem of the money easily. He decides to leave it hidden in the attic, for he concludes that life with the 500,000 francs would be exactly the same as before, perhaps in a more comfortable house, but one in which his family would continue its disorderly life. Henri inadvertently provides him with a solution to the other problem. When he offers to buy Charles's silence, Charles refuses to take anything. If he were to tell Henri that he had stolen the equivalent of 500,000 francs from him, Henri, although furious, would regain his assurance and overbearingness. Charles wants Henri to be as victimized and humiliated as he has always been and believes that Henri's inability to understand his refusal will produce this effect. "He alone prevented his brother-in-law from tranquilly enjoying his fortune and position! . . . And what made it even worse, precisely, was that he was so humble, so unobtrusive, so much a minor employee and poor relation!"[22] Charles has discovered the revenge of the underdog. In his office, he continues to wait for Henri and persists in saying nothing, "to make his brother-in-law die from fear, little by little.[23]

VI   *Illness as a Stimulus for Self-Appraisal*

While crime or antisocial behavior are the usual stimuli for the awakening of Simenon's middle-aged heroes, this is not always so. The protagonist of *Il y a encore des noisetiers* is induced to reevaluate his life when he receives a letter from his first wife who is dying of cancer. In *Les Anneaux de Bicêtre* and *Les Volets verts*, the protagonists' own illness leads them to take stock of their lives.

René Maugras *(Les Anneaux de Bicêtre)*, editor-in-chief of an important French newspaper, is struck with hemiplegia and brought to Bicêtre hospital. Although his mind has remained unaffected, half of his body is paralyzed and he cannot speak. Acutely depressed, he considers the world to which he no longer belongs and which he now observes as an outsider, wondering whether it was ever worth the trouble it entailed. Like so many of Simenon's protagonists, Maugras questions whether others really believe in their role, whether they are really satisfied with themselves, or whether their activities, like his own, are simply a form of escape. He attempts to evaluate the results of his fifty-four years, and his pitiful inventory, which includes his drunken father, two unsuccessful marriages, and an unloved daughter, proves to him that life is meaningless. François Mauriac has remarked that it is novels like this that succeed, where Christian sermons have failed, in convincing us of the vanity of life.[24]

Maugras's bitter conclusion is reinforced by the humiliations to which his body is subjected, and by his feelings of desperation, outrage, and helplessness as he is reduced by sickness to the status of an object:

An instrument forced his jaws apart, and a tube was thrust down his throat. He felt it going down. He wanted to signal to them that he was choking, that he couldn't bear it any longer, that he couldn't breathe. . . . Those ten or fifteen minutes were the most unpleasant he had ever experienced in his life. He had really felt just like an animal and he realized that he had behaved like one too, first by struggling, then, as he lay inert, by staring at each of them in turn with wild eyes. . . . They had hurt him badly, and above all they had taken away the little confidence he had left in himself and in man's potentialities.[25]

As he lies in his hospital bed, Maugras can think of only two moments when he seemed to have found a meaning in life, two moments during which he had felt "in harmony with nature. Twice he had almost been absorbed into nature. Nature had pervaded his whole being. He had become part of it. And both times he had been afraid,"[26] he had drawn back. Both of these experiences had been linked to water, sunshine, heat, and fresh smells. One took place on a Sunday in the country with his first wife and the other on a boat going to the island of Porquerolles:

When the boat slid away from its moorings, he stood in the bow, leaning over the transparent water. For a long time he was able to see down to the bottom and for the space of half an hour he lived in music, as though at the heart of a symphony.

That morning was like nothing he had ever experienced since. It was his great discovery of the world, of a boundless, radiant world of bright colors and thrilling sounds. . . . He had often been back to the Mediterranean seacoast. He had seen other seas equally blue, trees and flowers that were more extraordinary, but the magic had gone and of all his discoveries, this was the only one to have left a trace. . . .

Was twice in a lifetime enough?[27]

During the eight days in the hospital covered in the novel, Maugras changes from a dying man to a convalescent. He will return to his former life, knowing that for him there is nothing else, but with greater self-knowledge. He has reached no great conclusions, only a modest acceptance of his own inadequate, but terribly human self.

At the beginning of *Les Volets verts*, "the great Maugin," an aging French actor, is told by a specialist that, at the age of fifty-nine, he has the heart of a seventy-five year old man. The doctor's diagnosis provokes a great cry of weariness which he had been holding back for so long. "I am tired. T-i-r-e-d! Tired to death. . . .Do you understand?"[28] To the taxi driver who asks him where he wants to go when he leaves the doctor's office, he replies: "Anywhere! Anywhere else! Nowhere!"[29]

The novel traces the last weeks of Maugin's life, interwoven with flashbacks into his past. He had fled from a sordid background—his mother was the town whore and his father an alcoholic. He had worked all his life to become the greatest actor of his time. Now, confronted with death, he is aware that it is all unimportant, that he feels no pleasure at having achieved his goals. Simenon has remarked that neither the goal to be reached nor success are of any importance, but that it is "solely the energy we expend, and above all the enthusiasm we expend to reach it that count, no matter what the goal may be."[30] "I believe," he adds, "that this is more or less the case with every man who reaches or approaches his goal. He notices quickly that there was only one interesting thing: the pursuit of that goal. And, once having reached the goal, he is faced with a void. Consequently, why should he remain at any post to play the role of a marionnette? He now has but one objective: to find simple, down to earth joys . . . to cultivate his garden or to fish. . . . It all amounts to the same thing: to find nature once again and everyday life."[31]

Maugin leaves the theater to spend the time left to him fishing at St. Trophez. One day, he catches his foot on a fish hook and infection sets in. The doctors are unable to operate because of his heart. In his delirium, Maugin has a dream in which he is on trial. As he appears before his judges, he recognizes that:

He was guilty, without the shadow of a doubt. He knew it. He had, in a way, known it all his life. At least he had felt that he was somehow out of line, that something was wrong, something out of gear, something he was more or less consciously struggling against.

A little as though he had been swimming with all his might against a violent current to reach some invisible goal, the mainland, or an island, or simply a raft.

He blushed, ashamed. For he had been big and strong. . . . Yet, he had arrived nowhere. He had not attained his goal. . . . What was it that he had been guilty of? Was it to have chosen the wrong goal, to have wanted to be Maugin, always Maugin, a Maugin more and more important? He was going to explain the reason to them, and they would understand.

He had done that in order to escape. Yes! To escape, that was the word. He had spent his life trying to escape. . . . He had fled. . . . Lord God, how many things he had fled from, and how tired he was!

Was that it, at last? Was it the rule to remain, to accept?

Or was he guilty because he had spent his life looking for something that doesn't exist?[32]

Maugin's feelings of guilt and alienation are shared by the majority of Simenon's characters who are unable to break out of their solitude. All of them illustrate Camus's contention that, if no one is completely guilty, no one is completely innocent either. Armed with this understanding, Maigret refuses to judge. And that is why Simenon regards all of his characters with infinite compassion. As Maugin takes stock of his life, he realizes that the long road he has traveled has led nowhere. "He had climbed the slope too fast, and his heart could stand no more, missed a beat. . . . His body stiffened, as though he were trying to hold himself on his head and his heels, and suddenly he was filled with shame, felt tears welling up, couldn't find his hands to cover his face,"[33] as he stammered, just before dying: "Excuse me nurse. . . . I've dirtied my bed."[34]

VII   *One Who Succeeds*

The tears that linger on Maugin's eyelashes after he dies are symbolic of the failure of his life, while the bantering smile that remains on Bouvet's face *(L'Enterrement de Monsieur Bouvet)* even in death bears witness to his success in life. Even nature seems to be in harmony with him on the magnificent summer's day of his death:

The street-cleaning machine passed with the squeaking sound of its revolving broom which moved the water around on the pavement, and it seemed as if half of the roadway had been painted in dark colors. A large yellow dog had mounted a small white dog which remained immobile.

The old gentleman was wearing a light-colored, almost white jacket, like a colonial, and had a straw hat on his head.

Things assumed their places as if for an apotheosis. Against the sky, the towers of Notre-Dame were surrounded with a halo of heat and, up above, sparrows, supernumeraries which were almost invisible from the street, settled down among the gargoyles. A line of barges, with a tow-boat with a red and white triangle, had crossed all of Paris and the tow-boat lowered its smoke stack in greeting or to pass beneath the Pont Saint-Louis.

The sun spread out, luxurious and thick, fluid and golden like oil, making reflections on the Seine, on the pavement that had been wet by the street cleaner, on a skylight and on a slate roof, on the Île Saint-Louis; a secret, juicy life emanated from matter, the shadows were violet like on the canvases of the impressionists, the taxis on the white bridge were redder and the buses greener.

A light breeze transmitted a trembling to the leaves of a chestnut tree and all along the quais there was a quiver which approached by degrees, a refreshing, voluptuous breath that slightly raised the engravings fastened to the booksellers' stalls.

People had come from very far away, from the four corners of the world to live that moment. Buses were lined up on the square in front of Notre-Dame, and an excited, little man was speaking into a megaphone.

Closer to the old man, to the fat bookseller dressed in black, an American student was looking at the universe through the eye of his Leica.

Paris was immense and calm, almost silent, with splashes of light, sections of shadow in the proper places, sounds that penetrated the silence at opportune moments.

The old man with the light-colored jacket had opened a box filled with pictures and had leaned the box against the stone parapet in order to look at them.

The American student was wearing a red checked shirt and had no jacket.

The bookseller, seated on a folding chair, was moving her lips, without looking at her customer to whom she was talking in an endless stream. . . . She was knitting. Red wool slipped between her fingers.

The white dog bent her back beneath the weight of the large male dog who stuck out a wet tongue.

And then, when everything was in place, when the morning had reached an almost frightening degree of perfection, the old man died, without saying anything, without a moan, without a contortion, looking at his pictures, listening to the voice of the bookseller which continued to flow on, the chirping of the sparrows, the scattered horns of the taxis. [35]

The body of the old man, who was known to all the booksellers on the quai as M. Bouvet, is taken to his rooming house where his concierge lays out his body for burial. When the photo of M. Bouvet, taken by the American student, appears in the newspaper, those who once knew him appear, to reveal that Bouvet was the final incarnation of an amazing man who led many different lives. As the various layers of his life are peeled off, it becomes known that his name was Gaston Lamblot and that he was born to a wealthy family. He studied law in Paris but soon dropped out and lived with a young whore in the Latin Quarter where he frequented anarchist circles. When the girl's pimp attacked him with a knife for having stolen his livelihood, Gaston killed him in self-defense and fled to Belgium with the girl. After a year, he left the girl, as he would leave everything in turn, and went to England. During World War I, he was Agent Corsico, the best paid spy of the day. Serving as valet to the German ambassador, he was able to procure photographs of all the documents that passed through the safe of the German Embassy in Madrid while the ambassador enjoyed the orgies staged for him by Corsico. In 1918, "in a movement of revolt, fatigue, or disgust,"[36] he turned up in Panama in the guise of an American named Samuel Marsh, married there, and had a daughter. In Panama, he met a Belgian who told him about the Congo and its financial possibilities. He left his wife and child behind and set himself up on the border between Kenya and the Egyptian Sudan, where he amassed a fortune mining gold. Although he continued to send vast sums of money to his wife and daughter, he himself went native until, one day, he disappeared once again.

Despite his many flights, Bouvet was never able to give in to the temptation to become a tramp, the ultimate flight, because he could not tolerate alcohol. The "Professor," a teacher turned tramp, tells of his friendship with Bouvet and of Bouvet's longing to join him. "It's not easy to explain, and I'm not sure. He asked me questions. He watched me, watched the others . . . like me. [He wanted to find out] whether it was hard, whether sometimes I didn't want to lead some other kind of life. . . . I somehow got the idea that he'd have liked to come . . . with us."[37]

This theme of "longing for the street, for the gutter, to be the man who has nothing, possesses nothing, not even his neighbor's esteem, nothing on which to lean, who lives solely in, of, and by himself,"[38] appears in many of Simenon's novels. He, himself, has always been tempted to emulate those who have "the strength to flee completely, not to care a rap about what others think of them, of their position in the world, the strength to live in the gutter."[39]

At the end of the novel, Bouvet's various families permit his concierge, Madame Jeanne, to bury him as she had wanted, and the final pages are devoted to the funeral procession.

There were only a few women there, but there had been others in his life, including all the little Negro women of Ouélé whose children he had fathered.

He had left them, one after the other. He had taken off. He had spent his life leaving and this was now his last departure. . . . Mme Jeanne looked at the Professor with a knowing look. For, despite the fact that they were at the very end of the procession, they were just about the only ones M. Bouvet expected to have at his funeral.

He hadn't fled them. He had come to them. He had chosen them. The tramp's eyes were sparkling even more than the concierge's; *he* alone knew by how narrow a margin M. Bouvet hadn't run away one more time, hadn't come to search him out at the place Maubert or on the quais. It was as if he were the last link. Those in the first cars, whom they couldn't even see, represented past, almost forgotten periods and had only the importance that legal documents can confer. . . . A red truck passed them, got into the line, and, almost all the way to the cemetery where the prayers of intercession for the deceased were to take place in the chapel, the last car was separated from the others, as if it were not following the same funeral.[40]

VIII   Le Petit Saint—*Success without Flight*

The success of Bouvet's life is due to his constant evasion, while that of Petit Louis *(Le Petit Saint)* is a product of acceptance and serenity. In 1962, Pierre de Boisdeffre wrote that Simenon's readers were still waiting for him to give them the great novel in which he would show not only the "infinity of human solitude, but also the grandeur of human communion; not only the *libido* and the *destrudo*, but also the will to make something of oneself; a novel in which man could still be the product of his milieu, but where he would no longer be its prisoner because the choice that he, himself, would make, would, in the words of Sartre, become his destiny."[41]

Simenon produced such a novel, *Le Petit Saint*, in 1964. When he finished it, he exclaimed: "At long last I have done it! With each successive novel for at least twenty years, I have been trying to externalize a certain optimism that is in me, a joie de vivre, a delight in the immediate and simple communion with all that surrounds me, and to attain, in order to describe such a state, to some kind of serenity. However, after the first third or half, my earlier novels invariably turned into tragedy. For the first time, I was able to create, in *Le Petit Saint*, a perfectly serene character, in immediate contact with nature and life. That is why, if I were allowed to keep only one of all my novels, I would choose this one."[42]

Le Petit Saint takes its name from the epithet applied to the protagonist by his schoolmates because of his serene detachment and the "quiet and almost continuous satisfaction, that could have been taken for placidness, [which his smile reflected]. A gentle smile, without irony, without meanness, without aggressiveness, a smile that someone once compared to that of Saint Medard, whose church stood at the bottom of the street. He was happy, he watched, he went from one discovery to another, but . . . he made no effort to understand. He was content with contemplating a fly on the plaster wall or drops of water rolling down the windowpane."[43] What Louis observes, but transformed by his vision, is the poverty-stricken but vibrant life of the working class on the rue Mouffetard in Paris at the turn of the century. Little Louis lives in one room with his mother and four brothers and sisters, all sired by different men. The children sleep on mattresses lined up side by side on the floor, separated by a hanging sheet from the high walnut bed occupied by their mother and her current lover. The children observe their mother and her lovers through a hole in the sheet and their actions are copied incestuously by the oldest brother and sister. Louis "liked the room that was divided in half by the bedsheet that hung from a rod, he liked the smell of the mattresses lined up side by side, the portrait of his mother in a white veil and of a man with a blond mustache, the patches of wallpaper, particularly the one with the girl on a swing. He liked, above all, the warmth that the stove gave off in waves. in blasts, the way it roared at times, the glowing

ashes that suddenly collapsed into the drawer at the bottom."[44] The
feeling is one of warmth and security in that room in which they
live "with one another as in a burrow, sheltered from the outside
world, and come what may, their mother is there to protect
them."[45]

The mother is a warm woman, working hard for her children, getting up before dawn to push a cart across Paris to Les Halles to buy
the vegetables she resells from a pushcart in her neighborhood. She
takes things as they come, "enjoying what is good in life, contenting
herself uncomplainingly with what is less good, and ignoring the
rest as if it did not exist."[46]

Louis observes everything. He doesn't like people to bother him
or to ask him questions. He wants to be let alone to observe, smell,
and touch everything about him. He develops the habit of accom-
panying his mother to Les Halles:

There were vegetables, fruit, poultry, cases of eggs, everywhere, on the
sidewalks, in the gutter, all over the storehouses, and everything was moving, was heaped in one place and transported to another.
Figures were yelled. People were writing on black pads with violet pen-
cils. Market porters wearing big hats and carrying a side of beef on their
shoulders rushed through the streets. Tubs were overflowing with guts.
Women sitting on stools were plucking poultry with the rapidity of
magicians.
It all looked chaotic, but he would soon learn that, for all the apparent
disorder, every wagon, every crate, every cauliflower, every rabbit, every
man had a definite place and a precise job.[47]

Louis went "in order to renew the wonder of it, to complete his set
of exciting images, for example, that of the Seine. . . . He was constantly discovering images, yellow and green housefronts, sign-
boards, nooks crowded with barrels."[48] Louis notices that his
mother is not engrossed as he is in the spectacle of the street, but
even crosses the Seine at the Pont Saint-Michel without being
aware of the color of the light that day or whether there is a current
in the water, and never even looks at the towers of Notre-Dame.[49]

Louis's preoccupation with visual images prepares him for his
metamorphosis into a great painter. The images he stores up will
appear on his canvases, including those of the changes going on
around him: introduction of gas lighting into their room, anarchist
bombs, construction of the Métro, public works going on all over
Paris, electricity being installed everywhere. As Louis begins to

paint, he is haunted by the desire to employ pure colors. "He never felt that they were limpid enough, vibrant enough. He would have liked to see them quiver. . . . What he would have liked to get down on canvas was reality itself, as he saw it, or rather as it composed itself spontaneously in his mind."[50] He was constantly seeking to capture "a certain sparkle . . . the quivering space between objects."[51]

The last part of Louis's life is hastily sketched, for it was the development of his character and the discovery of his genius that were important. One of his brothers was killed in the Great War, his sister became fat and callous, another brother would die in prison, while still another brother lived with his wife in Ecuador and spent his time hunting .butterflies and birds of paradise. His mother remarried and lived comfortably thereafter. "Had he not taken something from everything and everyone? Had he not used their substance?"[52] Louis would wonder when asked about his success.

He didn't know, he mustn't know, otherwise he would be unable to carry on to the end.

He continued to walk with little steps, to smile.

"May I ask you, Maître," he was asked, "how you see yourself?"

He did not reflect very long. His face lit up for a moment as he said joyously and modestly:

"As a small boy."[53]

Louis's response provides the key to his harmonious life and explains how he differs from Simenon's other characters. He succeeds because he has never lost the young boy's love of all of life. Almost all of Simenon's protagonists have failed to remain faithful to the children they once were. One day, seized with a longing for a world like the one shown in picture books, they flee in search of innocence and childhood purity. Their defeat is thus inevitable. Louis, on the other hand, has never failed to see himself as a young boy, and his joyous vision corresponds to that of an age he has never left behind.

CHAPTER 6

Exotic Novels

I *Disintegration of Characters*

SIMENON'S protagonists are characterized in general by
an absence of will. A theme prevalent in his work is that of a
man who watches impotently as his life disintegrates. Scarcely does
a character appear than he collapses and crumples away.
Everything takes place without him, despite him, or against him; he
is destroyed before our eyes and doesn't understand what is
happening to him as he is carried off, not by a whirlwind, but by the
everyday disquiet of an almost immobile existence. Simenon
watches his characters go astray and descend toward the abyss
without doing anything to restrain them. They do not direct their
own lives, but stand helplessly by, shunted about by the vicissitudes
of life.[1] While this disintegration of the characters takes place in all
surroundings in Simenon's novels, the unmerciful rain, heat, insects, and diseases of the tropics destroy them more quickly and
relentlessly.

II Adventure's Failures

In a series of articles, *Les Ratés de l'aventure (Adventure's
Failures)*, published in *Paris-Soir* in 1935 and later in book form under the title *La Mauvaise étoile*, Simenon wrote about men whose
dreams of self-fulfillment and wealth had led them to the tropics.
They were men "who were greedy for a broader, freer, more
beautiful life and who did not hesitate to leave everything to court
adventure. They were adventurers in the best sense of the word."[2]
Simenon added that although he read that some had succeeded, he
never met them. He only met the others, the failures, reduced to a
deplorable state by the tropics. "Our gentle failures in France are
spoiled children beside these men who . . . aimed higher, much
further. And who descended in a vertical plunge."[3]

According to Simenon, if you do away with picturesque elements, most tropical adventures assume a tragic aspect, "a day to day tragedy, heavy as the sky, thick as the forest, a nightmarish tragedy, an oppression, the emptiness of the mind and the soul before a landscape that is always the same, that remains forever alien and where, nonetheless, you must die, knowing that there is in France a village, a city. . . ."[4]

In *L'Heure du Nègre*, a series of articles published after Simenon's return from Africa, he wrote:

. . .nature is sad. The African sun is a trap. It is grey, as implacable as a stormy sky. The virgin forest is also grey . . . the sadness of all of Africa, of the trees, rivers, animals, the sadness even emerges from the sight of the monstrous continent reproduced on a map.

The whites count for nothing there or rather they are the victims, because, while the blacks adjust to this bovine passivity, the Europeans die of it.

The master, the true master, the one who leads the black-skinned and white-skinned flocks, the animals and the plants, is Africa! Africa, which brutally ignites an implacable sun at six o'clock in the morning. Africa, which forbids you to stir on pain of death at certain hours of the day. Africa, which at six in the evening plunges you without transition into the feverish night! Africa and its rigorous seasons that dry up rivers or make torrents of them, kills a certain percentage of living beings at the equinox, crushes everything beneath its weight, its mass, its mathematical regularity, without ever permitting either relaxation or a semblance of free will. . . .

The Negro is accustomed to it. He knows how to see people die and how to die, whether from laying rails or from leprosy, sleeping sickness, the bite of a crocodile or a leopard.

The white man struggles desperately for his life and what he gains sometimes in the struggle is to go mad on time. They call it sunstroke, and they send him back to end his days in his native village.[5]

III   *Tropical Madness*

Madness is the destiny of Joseph Timar, the ill-fated protagonist of *Le Coup de lune*. He arrives in Gabon with the hopes, expectations, and luggage of a young man from a good family. There, he discovers that the company that hired him is on the verge of bankruptcy, that the job is a ten day's boat journey away in the heart of the forest, and that the company's boat is inoperative. Even were he to find a way to get there, his actions would be futile because the post is still occupied by a demented old man who

threatens to greet his replacement with a shot in the head. "Then, it
was no longer only the anguish of homesickness that gripped his
heart, it was the anguish of uselessness. Useless to be there! Useless
to struggle against the sun that penetrated all his pores. Useless to
swallow each evening that quinine that nauseated him! Useless to
live and to die to be buried in a makeshift cemetery by half-naked
Negroes."[6]

Timar is easily influenced by the proprietress of his hotel, Adèle,
who convinces him to use his influence to obtain a lumbering concession for which she will supply the capital. His association with
Adèle, whose shooting of a native boy has caused an uproar in the
colony, has cut him off from the colonial authorities. He and Adèle
go into the interior to the concession, and there heat, drink, fever,
and his own lack of will destroy him completely. After denouncing
Adèle as the murderer at a trial that had been rigged against a poor
native, Timar is shipped back to France, half mad, muttering: "But
there's no such place as Africa."[7]

Madness may also have been responsible for the death of the
young engineer that Simenon describes in the chapter of *La
Mauvaise étoile* entitled "The Man Who Fought Rats or the Most
Banal of Stories." The tragedy occurs at the height of the rainy
season:

For hours and for days on end, the rain falls in tepid sheets, inundates the
landscape and, as soon as the lemon-colored sun appears behind the solid
curtain of clouds, steam rises from the ground while human lungs dilate in
vain and breathing is difficult.

It is evening. Small streams of water have entered the hut and mildew
eats into the boots, covers everything made of leather. The papers spread
out on the desk are soft, like wet cloths. . . . The man, half naked because
of the heat which makes his skin glisten with sweat, writes as he pants, stopping after each sentence. . . . "You must act quickly, I beg of you. Let
D. . . bring me a large quantity of antiscorbutic syrup without delay and
an even larger quantity of parts. . . . Bed bugs, rats, stifling heat, sleepless
night. Here, the rats are winning. It is a real scalp dance. I have just killed
two, but there are one hundred of them and I dare not extinguish the
light. . . ."[8]

In this atmosphere, the engineer goes slightly mad. He contends
that the corporation that sent him out there is speculating on this
insignificant gold mine and has issued instructions that he be killed
rather than permitted to leave to reveal the truth to European in-

vestors. When he is found shot in the head, it appears to be a
suicide, but Simenon writes that he is not sure whether it is crime or
suicide. Companies have been known to commit greater crimes.
However, on the other hand, Simenon writes, "I'm not sure. I've
seen the country. I suffered from its glaucose sun and sweat
prevented me from writing several times."[9]

IV *Those Who Go Native*

While some go mad, others, like Joseph Dupuche *(Quartier
Nègre)*, sink into squalor and alcoholism. When Dupuche, a young,
well-bred provincial French engineer, arrives in Panama with his
bride of two weeks, he is optimistic about his future. However, he
discovers that the company that hired him in Paris has gone
bankrupt and his letters of credit are worthless. Alone and penniless
in Panama, the couple turns to the white community, which is composed in large part of ex-convicts and shady entrepreneurs.
Dupuche's wife, Germaine, is hired as cashier in the French-owned
hotel in Panama while he is lodged in the native quarter. Although
Germaine's refinement and charm endear her to her employers,
Dupuche is unable to win the battle against the sun, fever, and
alcohol. He begins to drink *chicha,* a drink prepared by Indian
women who chew corn for hours and spit it, mixed with their saliva,
into a receptacle of baked clay. Water is poured on it and it
ferments rapidly to produce the deadly beverage.[10] Dupuche discovers that he likes the poverty of the native quarter and has no
desire to return to France. His wife is a stranger. "It wasn't his fault
and perhaps it wasn't hers either. Perhaps they would have always
ignored the gulf between them if they hadn't suddenly found
themselves without a cent in a foreign country far from all possible
help. Who knows whether, without that, they would have spent
their whole lives thinking they loved one another?"[11]

Dupuche lives with a young native girl who deceives him
shamelessly. He begins to prowl around a section of the beach
where, only a few yards from buildings made of reinforced concrete,
a group of Negroes have returned to the way of life of their
ancestors in huts exactly like those found in the heart of Africa.
"Four families of Negro fishermen had camped there for years and
founded their own city which the law couldn't touch. . . . They
slept, they looked at the ocean. From time to time, they pushed a
dugout into the water and could be seen floating around in the
resplendence of the bay."[12]

Emulating these natives, Dupuche becomes indifferent to everything. *"He lived in himself!* He was sufficient unto himself."[13] When he walks in the street, he is elsewhere at the same time. He repels his wife's final advances and proposes divorce. He is disinterested in the rules of society and is happy with his black mistress, whose devotion is like that of a dumb animal. Dupuche dies ten years later of acute black-water fever after having realized his ambition "to live in a hut at the water's edge behind the railroad, among the rank weeds and the refuse. At that time he had six children, three of whom were dark skinned, two mestizos, and one, the youngest, almost white. . . ."[14]

V *Premature Death*

The third tragic destiny offered to the "failures of adventure" is an early death, either by one of the infinite forms it assumes in Africa, or by suicide. Oscar Donadieu dies a suicide in *Touriste de bananes.* "Banana tourist," Simenon explains in *La Mauvaise étoile,* is the contemptuous epithet applied to those of all classes and all countries who go to the tropics.

One fine day when they are disgusted with their mediocrity, or frightened by impending destitution, someone tells them: "In the islands, you can still live as if it were heaven on earth, without money, without clothes, without worrying about tomorrow. . . ." They sell everything to pay their passage. When they debark, the prudent authorities, who have often been burned before, require them to deposit enough money for their return fare. Do you understand?
    The next day, every good banana tourist has already bought a sarong and a straw hat. Half-naked, he goes off to the endless beaches. . . .
    He is evidently a bit astonished to see that the natives are wearing detachable collars and are riding bicycles and he is indignant when buses full of Kanaka Indians pass him on the road.[15]

However, after a month or two, tired of subsisting on bananas and coconuts, bored with this tête-à-tête with nature, he returns home.
    Oscar Donadieu, the protagonist of the novel *Touriste de bananes,* appeared for the first time in *Le Testament Donadieu,* where his flight from the ugliness and corruption of society began. When his father, a wealthy shipowner, was mysteriously drowned one night, the family fell apart. The scandals and sordid squabbles over his father's estate caused Oscar to run off to America to work on the construction of a dam at Great Hole City, where he could

sink into anonymity and routine and where nothing unexpected could occur to trouble his life. "Like the others, he was awakened by the siren and was with other workers like himself. All of them wore the same khaki shirts, the same boots, the same waterproof clothing. All swung their arms in the same way while walking toward the factory and then made an identical gesture of the right arm toward the handle of the time clock."[16]

Oscar had been forced to return to France when his sister killed his brother-in-law and herself. After the funeral, Oscar remained in France, where he became involved with a radical political group to which he gave his complete allegiance until the leaders ran off with the funds. In *Touriste de bananes*, he flees once again, this time to Tahiti, in his quest for purity. He is saddened by the pejorative epithet "banana tourist" applied to those who, "like him, dreamed of blending with nature, living intimately with it while renouncing the comforts of civilization."[17] All Oscar wanted was to escape from the crowd and to live a simple life, but there wasn't anyone to whom he could talk, no one to understand his hopes.

He came to Tahiti to seek innocence, but the sordidness and corruption he discovers there are a parody of what he originally fled from in La Rochelle. His progressive disillusionment is interwoven with a secondary plot that contributes to the tragic denouement of the novel. Ferdinand Lagre, the captain of a merchant ship who had formerly been employed by Oscar's father, has murdered one of his ship's officers in a fit of jealousy over a Tahitian prostitute named Tamatéa. The trial is presided over by Judge Isnard, who had been keeping the girl himself until his wife put an end to the affair. As he watches the rigged trial in which the verdict has been agreed upon in advance by the judge, the governor, the prosecutor, and the defense attorney, Oscar tries to put himself into Lagre's shoes, trying to understand the man who was separated from the others, as was Oscar himself, by a barrier of incomprehension. For, "when all was said and done, it was he, and he alone, who had killed a fellow man. He alone could know what it really meant, and how little to the point were all these tedious formalities and long-winded phrases."[18]

While observing the proceedings, Oscar becomes disgusted with his own failure to rise and denounce the trumped up trial. Those about him believe that he has become one of them, that he has finally learned how to play the game. In reality, he has decided that life is no longer possible. "Even if he started to drink, that wouldn't alter matters. He would become disgusted with himself one day or

another and it would be even worse. . . . It was better to get it
over with once and for all. It wasn't possible that he had done all he
had done to come to this. He mustn't. He mustn't accept at any
price. . . . He had persisted so all his life, since he was very small,
in searching for something beautiful. . . . To search for something
or to flee something else? He did not know. That was of no importance! Perhaps both. . . . "[19]

Fearing that he will become like the others, Oscar kills himself
after spending the night with Tamatéa. The hysterical shrieks of
Tamatéa, who has awakened in a pool of blood, convey the horror
of Simenon's tropical hell with the ever present sleazy bar-hotel run
by an escaped convict, the colonial club where the colonists drink
themselves into daily stupors, the intense heat, tropical fevers, deadly insects, and rats.

VI   *One Who Succeeds*

While Simenon wrote mainly about failures in *La Mauvaise
étoile*, he described one man who succeeded, not by escaping like
Bouvet, but by accepting life serenely, like the little saint. "In the
heart of the Congo," Simenon wrote, "I have another friend who
left one fine day with a small inheritance and who founded a model
plantation three hundred kilometers from the nearest village. He
lives there, the only white among three or four hundred blacks.
Elephants replace tractors there. He produces a substantial amount
of coffee. He built an infirmary and he takes care of his men and
delivers the women's babies. . . . Only, as he told me the evening
we dined together on his veranda, he just makes ends meet and he
will have to save for five or six years to pay for a trip to Europe."[20]

Ferdinand Graux, the "white man with glasses" *(Le Blanc à
lunettes)*, is patterned on this successful planter. However, unlike
petit Louis, whose serenity is never threatened, Graux must first go
through a crisis before acquiring inner peace. He is a French coffee
planter in the Belgian Congo, who is returning from home leave as
the novel opens. When he arrives at his plantation, he learns that a
private plane carrying a young English noblewoman, Lady Mackinson, and her friend, Captain Philps, the pilot, has made a forced
landing on his property. Lady Mackinson, whose knee is dislocated,
has been moved into Graux's house, while Captain Philps has been
attempting to have the plane repaired. Lady Mackinson belongs to
a group on which Simenon has always looked with disfavor, the

group that travels from one grand hotel to another and tries to escape its boredom through drugs, alcohol, and sexual promiscuity. Lady Mackinson's sexual freedom is misunderstood by Graux, who falls desperately in love with her after a night together. She is unaffected by their encounter and leaves without hesitation to join her husband and children in Constantinople, when the plane is repaired. Graux follows her.

During Graux's absence, his fiancée, Emmeline, alarmed by the tone of his letters which tell of a violent moral crisis, flies out to the Congo. She is the perfect companion for Graux, who chose her because her seriousness and calmness complemented his personality perfectly. She takes over the management of the plantation as she patiently awaits his return. At the same time, a young couple who had returned to the Congo on the same boat as Graux falls victim to the fate reserved for most of Simenon's colonial characters. The husband, driven mad by heat, drink, and failure, fires at his wife and kills himself. Almost as if their fate had exorcized the evil influence of the tropics, Simenon permits Graux to return. In the journal he kept of his flight, Graux wrote: "I wonder what would happen if I didn't possess an instinctive need for equilibrium. . . . What pushed me to come to Istanbul whatever the cost? I thought I was irresistibly driven toward catastrophe of one sort or another. . . . I even began to hallucinate, to think of mass murder. . . . I even thought myself capable of living forever in her wake. . . . Romanticism."[21]

As the novel ends, Graux and Emmeline are about to embark on a life of conjugal respect, affection, and understanding, exceptions to the rule of madness, suicide, and degradation.

VII *Simenon, the Story Teller*

While the story is secondary to the psychological analysis of the characters in most of Simenon's novels, many of them, particularly those set in the tropics, are exciting tales of adventure and suspense: *Le Passager du "Polarlys"* is a story of drug addiction, murder, storms at sea, and escape; *Les Pitard* tells of shipwreck and rescue at sea; *Les Gens d'en face* is a chilling portrayal of Soviet secret police activities in Batum; *Ceux de la soif* describes slow death from thirst in the Galapagos; *Long cours* incorporates many of the stories of murder, madness, and adventure described in *La Mauvaise étoile*; *Les Rescapés du "Télémaque"* tells of shipwreck and cannibalism;

Le Passager clandestin includes stowaways, suicide, and contested inheritances. In all of these novels, interest is centered on the plot, rather than on what the character thinks or feels.

The novella *Sous peine de mort* illustrates admirably the storyteller's gift. It opens on a note of suspense as Oscar Labro, the protagonist, receives another in the series of postcards he has been getting for seven months, each of which is postmarked closer and closer to Labro's island of Porquerolles and each one of which contains the message: "We'll finally meet, you scum. On pain of death, do you remember? Your old Jules."[22] The reader does not know why these cards so alarm Labro nor why he has given up his beloved fishing to go down to the dock morning after morning to meet the daily boat from the mainland. Finally, on the one hundred sixty-ninth day after receipt of the first letter, Jules arrives. When he debarks, it is apparent that he has a wooden leg. "M. Labro didn't move any more than would a rabbit hypnotized by a snake. They were a few meters from one another, one with only one leg and one with only one eye, and their outlines were similar: they were two men of the same age, of the same build, of the same strength."[23] When the people on the dock look at them, they feel instinctively that they have a score to settle.

Gradually, as the story continues, the reader learns that Labro was sent to Gabon by his employer when he was twenty-two years old, to the hottest and most unhealthy part of the jungle to arrange for the collecting of palm oil. For three days he had been battling the mosquitoes in the unbearably hot Umbolé swamp. All about him there were

canals, rivers of muddy water where large bubbles burst continually on the surface, where animals of all sorts swarmed. . . . And not a single small area of real solid ground, low banks covered with such dense vegetation that one could hardly penetrate it. Night and day, insects so ferocious that he lived most of the time with his face wrapped in mosquito netting beneath which he was suffocating. . . . You could travel for days without seeing a hut, a human being, and then it happened that he saw a dugout canoe between the roots of a mangrove tree and on this canoe there was a sign: "It is forbidden to swipe this craft on pain of death."[24]

The sign gave Oscar an idea. His men stank, his legs were stiff. Were he to take that canoe and tie it to the first, he would be alone for the remainder of the trip. His misery prompted him to steal the canoe, to write an obscenity on the sign, and to put his name to it.

Jules had discovered Labro's whereabouts when he read the announcement of his daughter's wedding in the newspaper and had come to carry out his threat. Day after day, Jules and Labro go fishing together as Jules tortures him with uncertainty about the day he has chosen for Labro's death. Each day, Jules has a new idea and confides in Labro, as one confides in a close friend, the various types of death he has envisioned for him. Labro lives in terror, unable to denounce Jules to the police because his only proof is the postcards, which the postmistress has already described as an adolescent hoax. He also has certain scruples. He is no longer the man who committed the crime for which he has never ceased to feel remorse. "That man, such as he was, was partially the result of what [he] had done."[25] But still he wonders whether he should permit himself to be killed, to live for weeks or even months with the thought that Jules might announce at any moment that the time had come. Jules sadistically plays on Labro's fears until, one day, he goes too far by asking Labro for suggestions on how to commit the perfect crime, thus giving him the idea of getting rid of Jules in the same way. One day, after a brief struggle in the boat, they overturn and Labro drowns Jules by knocking him unconscious.

Everyone on the island is pleased to be rid of the intruder, particularly the police, who reveal to Labro that he was not Jules, but a petty thief named Marelier who was sought by the police in five countries. For the last twenty years, he had been living dishonestly in North Africa and the Levant. Before that, he had spent ten years in prison and had lost his leg trying to escape, not in the Umbolé swamp of Gabon, as he had told Labro. He had never been to Gabon, he had never owned a canoe, he didn't even know how to swim; Oscar had killed for nothing. He had killed a "poor fellow who undoubtedly meant him no harm, a common thief who sought only, by threatening him from time to time, to sponge on him and to spend peaceful days in Porquerolles."[26]

Labro resumes his former life. "He had to get accustomed to being a murderer. . . . All that happened because some crook or other, who was tired of wandering around the world pursued by the police, had heard one day in a bar, God knows where, colonials tell the story of the dugout. . . . And also because that crook, one day in Addis-Ababa, had got hold of [the newspaper] *Le Petit Var*, and had read Oscar Labro's name there. And that had given him the idea of ending his days in peace on the island of Porquerolles."[27]

Because *Sous peine de mort* is primarily a story in which the events are more important than the characters, Oscar's emotions are mentioned only in passing. His guilt is a simple guilt over a definite act, one for which he feels he must pay, not the cosmic disquiet of the majority of Simenon's protagonists. We know, too, that he will be able to rationalize his murder as part of the struggle for survival and that he will not only become "accustomed to being a murderer," but will also, in time, cease to think about it.

CHAPTER 7

The Novelist and the Art of the Novel

I The "Pure" Novel

IN a speech entitled *Le Roman de l'homme*, of 1958, Simenon discussed two questions that had always preoccupied him—why do so many people choose the profession of novelist, which generally leads nowhere, and why do so many others read novels to the exclusion of all other forms of literature? His answer to the first question, that writing is a means of relieving unbearable inner tension, led him to define the novel as "a passion that completely possesses and enslaves the writer and that permits him to exorcize his demons by giving them a form and casting them out into the world."[1]

Simenon added that the popularity of the novel can be attributed to the fact that it satisfies an equally great need in the reader, who is not seeking in it an escape from reality, but is attempting to see whether others are prey to the same passions, the same doubts, the same vices, the same temptations, the same discouragements as he. When he discovers that others are like him, he is less ashamed of himself and regains confidence in life. Because people today lack a strong religion and a firm social hierarchy, they are more insecure than heretofore. That is why modern novels do not provide a comforting view of humanity, but present it as it really is. "Other periods have left us the novel of the clothed man, of the man on parade. Will ours give us the portrait of the naked man, the one who looks at himself in the mirror while shaving and has no illusions about himself?. . . . Is he less great in his search for equilibrium, in his thirst for truth, than his ancestors who draped themselves in purple and affected a borrowed serenity?"[2]

To illustrate the difference between the modern novel and the novel of yesterday, Simenon wrote: "You may show the first ten months in the relationship of two lovers, as in the literature of long ago. Then, there is a second kind of story in which they begin to get bored and that was the literature of the end of the nineteenth century. But, in the third story, the man is fifty and tries to have another life, the woman becomes jealous, children are involved. The modern novel doesn't end when the lovers marry, it doesn't end when they get bored, but goes even further to show the characters driven to their limit."[3]

The modern novel, for Simenon, is the tragedy of our day and, like those of ancient Greece, poses the basic problem of man's destiny. Simenon has called his novels "romans-tragédie" (tragedy-novels) and in them he has adopted many of the rules that governed the ancient tragedies. Like them, his novels start at the moment of crisis and lead rapidly and inexorably to a tragic conclusion. There are no long introductions or chronological expositions in his novels; the past is evoked rapidly in a series of flashbacks. There are few characters and no subplots, action is limited and attention is focused on the eternal drama of man's existence. What Simenon is trying to produce is the quintessential, or "pure," novel, reduced to its basic elements and containing nothing that can be depicted through other media. Simenon believes that the domain of the novel has shrunk, since other means of expression have taken over the picturesque, philosophy, and psychology. Thanks to mass communication, the reader's horizon has become so enlarged that excessive detail is no longer necessary. Having renounced all claims to journalism or teaching, the modern novelist should be able to suggest a setting, evoke an atmosphere with a few brief strokes, and then concentrate on the crisis that pits man against destiny.

II   Atmosphere

Simenon has mentioned that he believes that what critics call his atmosphere is nothing more than the impressionism of the painter adapted to literature. Like the impressionists, he tries to give weight to his impressions:

A commercial painter paints flat; you can put your finger through. But a painter—for example, an apple by Cezanne has weight. With just three strokes. I tried to give to my words just the weight that a stroke of Cezanne's gave to an apple. That is why most of the time I use concrete words. I try to avoid abstract words. Or poetical words, you know, like *crépuscule* [twilight], for example. You don't feel them. Whereas the word *pluie*[rain] is material, you lose all the materiality of the rain if you speak of *ondée* [heavy shower]. I try to use only material words and, even to express ideas, I force myself to do so with concrete rather than abstract words.[4]

Using only concrete words, Simenon is able to convey the atmosphere of the city of Liége in his youth during the German occupation:

But the story of the occupation can't be told any more than the story of the inflation. It is not made up of facts: it is an atmosphere, a state of being, a barracks smell in the streets, the moving blob of unfamiliar uniforms, it is marks which replace francs in your pockets, and the preoccupation with eating that replaces all others, it is new words, unfamiliar music, and mobile soup kitchens along the sidewalks; it is the habit the eye falls into of looking for the new handbill on the board which tells the hour after which it is forbidden to circulate in the streets or which announces a new consignment of sugar at the food supply center, or else the necessity for all men over eighteen years of age to present themselves to the Kommandatur, unless the handbill is red and lists the names of recently executed civilians.[5]

Simenon excels in conveying a few decisive sensory impressions that evoke an atmosphere more vividly than any long itemized description. A spot of sunlight on his desk reminds the bourgemestre of Furnes of the jetty at Ostend with its sand "the color of blond tobacco, the changing sea that always remains pale, the parasols, the light dresses on the benches, on the rented chairs, the children running, the large red rubber balls that hit you in the legs."[6] While his images are primarily visual, Simenon often establishes relationships between diverse sensory impressions. Maigret, tracking a criminal, sees the dawn break: "He saw the first anglers settle themselves on the banks of the river from which a fine mist was rising; he saw the first barges bottled up at the locks and the smoke that was beginning to rise from the houses in a sky the color of mother of pearl. . . . It was amusing after the night he had just spent to walk in the grass which was wet with dew, to smell the odors of the earth, that of the logs that were burning in the fireplace, to see the maid, who had not yet done her hair, come and go in the kitchen."[7]

A description of evening on the island of Porquerolles similarly blends olfactory and visual impressions. "The air had a curious odor at that time. The sea also. The sea above all. And the universe was of an extraordinary color. Everything was light, almost pale, but of a luminous paleness. Pale blue. Pale green. Even the bright colors of the boats had an astonishing lightness. Everything was wrapped in a light vapor."[8]

Sensory impressions are also used to express states of being, both physical and mental. Simenon uses olfactory impressions in the following passage to convey the special poverty of Porquerolles: "Perhaps it was true that you could still smell the odor of sweat, but it was mixed with other odors that were both bitter and muted, children's urine and sour milk, the smell of garlic, of fish, at the same time as that odor that came from the pine forests and the arbutus, which was sort of the smell of the island."[9]

The sound of church bells, often linked with images of the sea, more often with Sundays, constitutes a leitmotif in Simenon's work. By a remarkable process of synaesthesia, Simenon uses visual images to evoke the sound of these bells:[10]

It was Sunday to such an extent that it was almost disgusting. Maigret claimed half seriously, half jokingly, that he had always been able to scent Sundays from his bed without even having to open his eyes.

Here, something unexpected was taking place with the bells. They were real church bells, however, but faint and thin like those of chapels or of convents. You were bound to believe that the quality, the density of the air was not the same here as elsewhere. You clearly heard the hammer strike the bronze, which gave forth a small, nondescript note, but it was then that the phenomenon began: a first ring took shape against the pale sky which was still cool, stretched out, hesitating like a smoke ring, became a perfect circle from which other circles magically came forth. The circles, ever larger and ever purer, passed beyond the square, the houses, stretched out above the port and far off over the sea where little boats were rocking. You felt them above the hills and the rocks and they still had not ceased to be perceptible when the hammer struck the metal once again and other sonorous circles came forth, to recreate themselves, then still others that you listened to with the same innocent amazement as when you watch fireworks.[11]

A critic has pointed out that the sense of touch is so important in Simenon's work that he even invented a new word, or rather transformed an adjective "mouillé" (wet, damp, moist) into the more concrete noun "le mouillé" to signify something indefinable and omnipresent in his work. It is neither rain, nor fog, but something more tenacious, so that you have a face "caked with mouillé," a "night of mouillé," a boat floundering "somewhere in the mouillé."[12]

Climate plays an important role in the creation of Simenon's atmosphere. In Northern Europe, it rains continually. "It had never rained so much. The drops pattered on the sidewalks like celluloid balls and water came out from everywhere, from the gutters on the roofs, sewers, one might even say from beneath the door, forming sheets of water that automobiles entered with caution. . . . No sky, no depth to the atmosphere, no color. Nothing but icy water."[13] On the Côte d'Azur and the island of Porquerolles, "the sun weighs down. Everything requires an effort, an effort to adapt, to understand. . . . The air is thick and heavy. The ground, trees, walls steam, emitting waves of heat."[14] Between Hamburg and La Rochelle, the climate is changeable as in all temperate regions.[15] And, in the exotic novels, the intense, debilitating, suffocating sun alternates with the intolerable rainy season, a climate in which "you must live in slow motion, calculate your slightest gesture in order to survive."[16]

In the American novels, there is the parched Arizona desert and the "luminous mist that rose from the desert of sand . . . the ever-changing colors on the mountains that seemed, far off, to close in the world on all sides."[17] Or else, the swollen Santa Cruz river, the real protagonist of *Le Fond de la bouteille,* during the rainy season when it was "high, already higher than during the night. It formed a dark yellow mass, flowing slimy and thick, heaving in places, breathing like a beast, carrying along tree trunks, empty cans, all kinds of filth. . . . "[18] *La Mort de Belle* opens as cars make fresh tracks in the newly fallen snow in a small Connecticut town, while *Les Frères Rico* provides an unforgettable impression of the sea at sunrise in Miami: "The sea was calm. All he heard was one small wave, the one which, forming not far offshore in a barely perceptible undulation, rolled onto the sand, in a sparkling curl and churned up thousands of shells."[19]

Above all, in more than seventy novels, it is Paris in all seasons. The cold November rain falls "from a sky of low, unbroken grey, one of those steady showers that seem wetter and somehow more perfidious, especially the first thing in the morning, than ordinary rain."[20] On a cold, wet, and dismal day in early March at eleven in the morning, "the offices were still bathed in a melancholy half-light, reminding one of an execution at dawn. At noon, the lights were still on and at three o'clock dusk had fallen again. Water was everywhere, the floor had puddles. People were incapable of saying three consecutive words without blowing their noses. All the newspapers printed photographs of suburbanites going home in rowboats through streets that had become rivers."[21] The Parisian winter sky, "in keeping with their consciences and their spirits, was a dull grey, more or less the same grey as the pavements. There was a chill in the air . . . an unpleasant chill. . . . The radiators in the offices were burning hot, making the atmosphere closer than ever, and from time to time there were gurgling sounds in the pipes, mysterious noises that came from the boiler room."[22] On a beautiful spring morning in Paris, Maigret feels young again,

due undoubtedly to the quality of the air, to its luminosity. There had been a morning exactly like it, mornings like it, when Maigret, who was a young inspector newly appointed to the Police Judiciaire . . . walked up and down the streets of Paris from morning until evening. Although it was already March 25, it was the first real day of spring, all the more limpid since there had been a downpour during the night accompanied by far off peals of thunder. For the first time that year, also, Maigret had left his overcoat in the closet in his office and, from time to time, the breeze puffed out his unbuttoned jacket.[23]

On a day in August, Maigret glances out of his window

at the motionless leaves on the trees on the Quai des Orfèvres, and at the Seine, which was flat and smooth as silk. . . . Every day toward early evening, for almost a week now, a brief but violent storm, accompanied by lashing rain, had sent the people in the streets scurrying in for shelter in doorways. These storms dissipated the intense heat of the day, and the cooler evenings that followed were a welcome relief. Paris was empty. Even the street noises were different, with intervals almost of silence. . . . On the streets at this time of year, it was almost a shock to hear someone speaking French.[24]

Simenon brings to the reader his Paris of blood puddings and brioches, Les Halles and onion soup, chestnut venders and anglers on the banks of the Seine, book dealers along the quais, bistros with zinc bars, Notre-Dame and the Île Saint-Louis, the Place du Tertre and the Place des Abbesses, the Moulin Rouge and Montparnasse, the Boulevard Saint-Michel and the Boulevard Rochechouart, the odors of café au lait, warm croissants, anisette, the small cafés and the elegant cafés of the Champs-Elysées, the rue Mouffetard and the Place Blanche, the whores and the drab hotels of Pigalle, the train stations, the Quai des Orfèvres and the Sacré-Coeur; a Paris that is constantly being torn down to provide underground parking for the cars that are strangling the city; a Paris that is struggling against the forces of progress and that will remain intact in Simenon's work when the battle has been lost.

It is this total recall of every mood and every aspect of Paris and of France, of Northern Europe, Africa, Tahiti, the Galapagos between the two great wars that has caused George Steiner to remark, in *Language and Silence*, that "Simenon may be among the last to have taken an entire culture for his verbal canvas."[25]

III   La Mort d'Auguste

La Mort d'Auguste portrays a segment of Simenon's Paris that has all but disappeared, the restaurant that brings together provincial and city life. Auguste Mature, who founded the restaurant in 1913 when he was twenty-six years old, named it L'Auvergnat after his native Auvergne. It is on a shabby side street in the neighborhood of the former Paris central market, Les Halles. Although it has flourished since the Second World War, its external appearance has not altered considerably. It is distinguished from the other restaurants in the area by the large hams and salamis that hang in the window and the large loaves of bread piled up, which Auguste still receives from his native province. The interior, however, has been enlarged and the decor reflects the popularity of the restaurant. Three Utrillos, which Auguste had obtained from a friend who was unable to repay a loan, hang on the wall. The paintings evoke the years of Auguste's youth, when starving artists bartered works that were to become priceless for a square meal.

The novel opens on a night in 1966 when a young, newly married couple enters the restaurant, deceived by its external simplicity. They are observed with disinterest by Antoine, Auguste's son who has been his partner since 1945, and Fernande, Antoine's wife, the cashier. Antoine doesn't bother to leave the back room for such unimportant clients, but has one of the waiters seat them at a bad table in the middle of the restaurant. Antoine reflects that the restaurant business is a funny trade:

They were like actors on stage. For hours on end each day, his wife and he could hardly exchange a glance or a few mumbled words. One had to smile, to listen to funny stories and to confidences.

At the age of forty-nine, he already was beginning to have the same gait as old Joseph. Most headwaiters and waiters, most restaurant owners, end up with flat feet.

The world around them is not the same world other people see. It is a world of numbered tables, of faces one knows or doesn't know, of menus, of certain specialties, of bills.

For the last twenty years, he had seen on the same hors-d'oeuvres cart, in the same order, the same concoctions with fancy names that gave them their gourmet appeal.

His gesture of presenting the menu never varied, nor the pantomime of preciously pouring the first drops of gamay d'Auvergne, of chanturgues, of white rosé de Corent or Sauvagnat into the host's glass.

The customer then took a little sip of the liquid, pretending to be a connoisseur who really knew his wines, clicked his tongue, and gave him a conspiratorial wink.[26]

In this brief opening scene, Simenon uses a few verbal strokes to convey the cold, calculating snobbery of certain restauranteurs. The reader's immediate dislike for Antoine and Fernande was a reaction intended by Simenon, who explained that all such effects are produced by the order of presentation and the movement of the sentence. "I have always tried," he explained, "to perfect a style that conveyed movement, that was all movement. Suppose that someone enters this room, takes off his hat, his gloves, opens his mouth to say something. According to the order in which you describe these gestures, you are going to have a different picture of the character. If he takes off his hat first and his gloves next, you do not have the same image of him as if he had done the reverse. The order of words in a sentence is of capital importance, of greater importance, in my opinion, than a refined syntax."[27]

Soon after the arrival of the young couple, the British ambassador arrives with a party of eight to whom he is showing off his "find," while old Auguste strolls from table to table, chatting with all regardless of social position, as he has always done since he and his restaurant were young. Suddenly, as he is telling the young married couple the story of his success, Auguste collapses at their table, dragging to the floor with him the red and white checked tablecloth to which he is clinging. He is carried upstairs to his bed in the apartment he occupies on the floor above the restaurant with his senile wife. Although she has ceased to recognize him, Auguste, who still loves her, continues to share with her the bed they bought when they were married. "He had not spent a single night away from her ever since they had been married, and even in recent times, when she looked at him as if he were a stranger or pet dog, he would often sit down in front of her in the hope that they might pick up the thread of God knows what conversation."[28]

Auguste dies during the night, and his death is the incident that triggers both the search for his missing will and the character portrayal of his three sons. In this work there is no dramatic conflict, because here, as in all of his novels, Simenon paints inner states of being and tensions rather than dramatic action. The reader learns about the brothers gradually, as he would in life. Ferdinand, the oldest, is a lawyer who has always been ashamed of the restaurant, but now is anxious to find out how much of his father's estate he can expect to inherit. He had always been relieved that Antoine had stayed with their parents and relieved him of the responsibility. But, now that his father has died, he wants to make sure that Antoine does not behave as if he were specially privileged. When he hears the extent of Auguste's wealth, he starts to think about what he would do if he were to retire. He had always thought his life was satisfactory, even enviable, but he suddenly realizes that it is empty, that he has no passions or hobbies. He is horrified to think that Antoine has become wealthy in the family business, neglecting to consider that Antoine had earned his money running the restaurant and that it was he who had brought about the success of the establishment.

Bernard, the youngest son, fat and spoiled and always short of money, is the black sheep of the family. His "irresolute face revealed the child of long ago, the young man who was at ease nowhere, the maturing man who had not managed to find his place in the world."[29] Antoine, the middle son, had let himself be talked into joining his father when he returned from a German prisoner of war camp after the war. It was a small restaurant then, his mother did the cooking and there was one waiter. Antoine and his father had drawn up a written agreement: "The moment before they were still a father and son standing next to each other and watching the traffic in the street. But, the moment Antoine gave his answer, the relationship between the two men changed. As naturally as can be, they became partners, accomplices of a sort, and the difference in age ceased to exist."[30]

As the search for Auguste's missing fortune goes on, Antoine discovers not only the character deficiencies of his brothers, but also that they had always resented him, that the attitude, tone, and look on Bernard's face were expressions "not of a momentary bitterness, but of a hatred that had matured over the years."[31] The search is difficult because nothing is known about Auguste's affairs; he had brought with him from the provinces the peasant's cunning and reticence in money matters. Antoine discovers ultimately that

Auguste had had a "business adviser," a man in whom he had complete confidence because he was also from the Auvergne. Auguste's trust had been misplaced, the adviser had died in prison where he had been sent for fraud. In Auguste's wallet, they find a few objects which are, in a sense, keys to his character: a safe deposit key, a prescription for reading glasses which his pride had prevented him from filling, photos of his three sons and of his wife at the age of sixteen, the way he saw her until his death.

The three brothers go to the safe deposit box and find that all the stocks it contains are worthless. Because Auguste had imagined he would be leaving a fortune to his sons, he had never spoken to them about money. He had wanted to surprise them. When he discovered the truth, he did not lodge a complaint against the dishonest adviser because to have done so would have been to admit that he was naive and to let his sons know that he was not leaving them the inheritance they anticipated. "He had worked all his life, ever since the age of twelve, to accumulate a fortune, counting every penny, and all that remained of it was the restaurant, which was really run by Antoine. . . . He had lived for months with a sense of shame, knowing that when he was gone he would leave behind him bitterness instead of regret. Antoine had the feeling that he had never understood his father so well, his peasant character, his humbleness and pride."[32]

Antoine permits his brothers to divide up the cash they found in the box, the last payment he had made to his father. He leaves them together in the restaurant, because "he had no desire to be present when the money was divided amidst the glasses on the table, beneath the eyes of the indifferent waiter."[33] The initial dislike that the reader felt for Antoine has given way in the course of the novel to sympathy, even admiration. This is in accord with Simenon's technique, which attempts to reproduce the rhythm of life in which you meet a person, react to his social personality, and then learn, as you penetrate beneath the surface, what the person is really like. The novel also conforms to Simenon's description of the modern novel in which there is "never a story in the traditional sense of the word, but merely the presentation of a moment of varying duration in the life of a man. It doesn't matter whether the events in the novel are dramatic or mundane, since the only thing that does matter is man himself, man and his relationship with the world, that is to say with life."[34]

IV *The Creative Process*

Simenon has described the way in which he goes about writing a novel. The creative process is set in motion one day when he begins to feel great anxiety and realizes that he will be virtually ill until he is able to effect a catharsis by means of the novel. "One day I become peevish, dissatisfied with myself . . . then I am not mistaken, I *need* to write."[35] At this point, a series of actions occurs that is invariable. First, Simenon rids himself of all social and family responsibilities for ten days and goes off alone, seeking to put himself into what he calls a "state of grace," which means to empty himself "of all preoccupations that personally affect [him], the man called Simenon, so as to become a sort of sponge that can absorb other people's personalities, live through other people's memories, and finally bring them out again—breathe them out—in the form of literature."[36]

While in this state, he will be receptive to some sensory impression that will recall an atmosphere from his past. For example, on a sunny day, he may remember a certain spring in the French provinces or in Arizona. A particular sound, an odor, will plunge him into the past evoking certain memories:

The day is ending. . . . It is the best time of day. . . . The contours of things become blurred, an ordinary street corner, the dark entrance to a house, a reflection on a wet pavement, everything easily takes on a mysterious aspect. That reminds me of ten, fifty small cities in which I roamed in the same way, and then it happens, by degrees memories come crowding back and move me. A certain small café in Dunkerque, one autumn evening, with its fishermen who looked as if they were sculpted in their slickers glistening with salt water. . . . There was sawdust on the floor and the men had at their feet the few fish they had kept for their evening meal. . . . A detail which still comes back to me: the cuckoo clock. . . . It made me jump at exactly six o'clock . . . the smell of spirits, of the alcohol which they call there "fil en six." Didn't these men hail from a boat named the Marie-Jeanne?

It would be good to live among them for a few days. . . . As a matter of fact, there was one of them, P'tit Louis, who, when he was drunk, and he was drunk every night, chewed glass and swallowed it. . . . He did the Newfoundland route on sailboats. . . . Six months at sea, a hard, frugal life. . . . He came ashore with a small store of money and, each time, he promised himself that he would go to see his old folks in Brittany the next day. Now, the next day, he would be lying dead drunk, in a gutter or on the benches of the police station. Three days, four days later, he didn't have a cent, not even enough to take the train, and he signed another contract, embarking for six more months of sea and continence.

P'tit Louis. . . . The others. . . . Dunkerque.[37]

Simenon's evocation of the sights, sounds, and smells of the fisherman's café was to provide the setting for *Au Rendez-vous des Terre-Nuevas*. The idea for *Le Président*, however, was provided by a purely visual impression. Simenon saw a black and white etching over a mantel that reminded him of Normandy and of a period he spent there years before with a woman. While this memory could have been the start of a love story, something diverted Simenon, as he also remembered an old house on a cliff that he had seen there and the curiosity he felt about its occupants. For some undetermined reason, he then thought of Georges Clemenceau and decided to write about an old man living in such a house, looking back on his life.[38]

After the setting, the protagonist is created, generally a composite of many people with whom the author came into contact. Simenon then gives him a name, a family, and a house, and he does this by consulting the morè than 150 telephone books for all countries that he keeps in his study. Contrary to usual practice, Simenon did not give a name to the Premier because he did not want to use a fictitious name for a supposedly real politician. Generally, however, he writes the name he has chosen on a yellow envelope—the rites Simenon follows are as rigid as those observed by his protagonists—and adds to the name the protagonist's telephone number, his address, his father's age if alive, his mother's age, his children, wife, friends, and so forth. He often also sketches a rough plan of the character's house, for he wants to know whether he opens the door to the left or the right when he gets home.[39]

Having decided to forego a name in *Le Président* and refer to the protagonist merely as the Premier, Simenon determined that he should be of peasant stock, born in Evreux, an industrial town in Normandy. Following extensive research on Evreux, Simenon then considered the household the Premier would have. He concluded that the old man would require a nurse, because he was eighty-two years old, as well as a secretary, cook, maid, and chauffeur. The chauffeur would also be a part-time spy, since the government, Simenon felt, would want to keep an eye on such a political "monument."[40] Each of the secondary characters was then given a complete identity, a procedure Simenon always follows, although he usually does not make use of this material.

"What does an old man like the Premier do to occupy his time?" was the next question. Simenon decided that such a man would surely be writing his memoirs. In the novel, Simenon has him write them on little pieces of paper which he hides from his staff all over the house. Such a man would also be jealous of the younger men coming to power. In *Le Président*, he is particularly jealous of a man named Chalamont who had once worked for him and who he had hoped would be his political heir, but who had long ago betrayed the Premier and his country by revealing to an unscrupulous speculator the government's secret plans to devalue the franc.

The problem that arises next for Simenon in writing a novel is crucial in its development. "I have such a man, such a woman, in such surroundings. What can happen to oblige them to go to their limit? That's the question. It will be sometimes a very simple incident, anything that will change their lives."[41] The incident, or catalyst, triggering this reaction, states Simenon, is the only contrived part of the novel, the rest follows inevitably. At this point, Simenon becomes the protagonist:

On the eve of the first day, I know what will happen in the first chapter. Then, day after day, chapter after chapter, I find what will come later. After I have started a novel, I write a chapter each day, without ever missing a day. Because it is a strain, I have to keep pace with the novel. If, for example, I am ill for forty-eight hours, I will have to throw away the precious chapters. And I will never return to that novel. . . . [I am the same character all the way through the writing of that novel.] Always, because most of my novels show what happens around one character. The other characters are always seen by one character. So it is in this character's skin that I must be. And it is almost unbearable after five or six days. That is one of the reasons my novels are so short; after eleven days I can't—it's impossible. . . . I am too tired.[42]

The fall of the government is the determining event in *Le Président*. Chalamont has been asked to form a new government. The old man can destroy his chances with a single telephone call. The Premier deceives himself into believing that his hour has finally come, that Chalamont will come to beg for his silence and his forgiveness. But Chalamont never contacts him, and the disappointed, disillusioned Premier soon understands why. The members of his staff have stolen the single weapon he still possessed, Chalamont's letter of confession. Once his anger has subsided, the Premier realizes that his perspective has changed, he has begun to see the vanity of all human endeavor and to look upon life with detachment. He decides to burn all remaining incriminating papers and looks toward death with serenity.

It was a strange impression, agreeable and a little terrifying, not needing to think any longer.

A few more flames, a few pages writhing and then falling to ashes between the tongs, and all threads would be severed.

"Are you asleep?" Milleran inquired anxiously, noticing all of a sudden that his eyes were closed. . . .

"No, my child."

He added, after a moment's silence: "Not yet."[43]

Here, as in all of Simenon's works, the settling of accounts is a private one. While Simenon has often been compared with Balzac, this is the great difference between the two novelists. Balzac's hero would have made the call to Paris to bring about a great scene of "annihilation," or, alternatively, would have brought the two men face to face for a confrontation.[44] An even more significant distinction is Simenon's refusal to pass judgment. While Balzac's readers would have been called upon to join the author in condemning political corruption, Simenon's readers are struck by his refusal to moralize. For Simenon, there are only problems, no answers.

CHAPTER 8

Conclusion

S IMENON'S decision in 1972 to stop writing novels provided a rare opportunity to consider the work of a living writer in its entirety. It was possible, from the perspective of a completed body of work, to study the author's narrative genius as well as his psychological perceptions as they apply to all of his novels. There are, inevitably, weak spots in such a vast literary production, principally certain works that seem to be hastily conceived imitations of earlier novels. *L'Homme au petit chien,* for example, is vastly inferior to *Le Temps d'Anaïs,* which it copies closely. Yet, even in this work, there are unforgettable passages, poetic transmutations of hideous reality that evoke the genius of Baudelaire.

Considered as a whole, Simenon's work is unique in modern literature. There are few contemporary writers who have recreated an entire period as completely as Simenon. He has evoked the atmosphere of France in the first half of the century, portraying its provinces and cities, its people and customs on a vast canvas that can be compared to Balzac's *Comédie humaine,* while, at the same time, imbuing the characters with a universality that transcends time and geographical boundaries. His novels form a bridge between the traditional novel, which sought merely to tell a story, and the modern novel, which has more ambitious goals.

Like the traditional novelist, Simenon keeps to chronological plot structure; his novels start at the moment of crisis—the past is evoked by a series of flashbacks—and work directly to a conclusion. Transitions between dream and reality, between supposition and fact are clearly indicated, and characters are easily distinguishable from one another. Simenon employs many traditional plot situations in his novels, such as conflict over an inheritance, desperate actions to maintain a privileged position, sibling rivalry leading to murder. The novels range in mood from tragedy to tragicomedy, to drama, to melodrama. That none of them is a comedy may be attributed to

Simenon's view of life, summed up in the words: "It's a difficult job to be a man."

Unlike many novelists of the post - World War II era, Simenon excludes from his work religion, politics, war, history, and metaphysical speculation. His aim, using a contemporary, timeless background, is to explore the eternal problems of man's destiny. For Simenon, success as a novelist implies being understood by people in all walks of life at all times.

Nevertheless, Simenon's novels are very distinctly products of the twentieth century. His impatience with language, his belief that watching one's language distorts thought and that language is a means, not an end, are attitudes shared by the majority of his peers. His novels also express the anguish of the twentieth century, the feelings of alienation, guilt, and expatriation to which the works of Kafka and Camus have accustomed us. Like their protagonists, as well as those of Sartre and Malraux, Simenon's characters find themselves alone in a world without transcendent values and without the social structure and hierarchy that formerly gave order, stability, and meaning to life. They are existentialists inadvertently, for they must find in themselves the answers that were formerly supplied by society and religion; they must act instinctively as they encounter each new situation, for nothing in their past dictates their actions.

Yet Simenon's protagonists go beyond those of Sartre and Camus to join those of Beckett. Unlike the existentialist heroes, Simenon's characters lack lucidity, they are unable to understand their desperate situation. The existentialist hero assumes his role and, by choosing, creates his essence. Simenon's characters, on the contrary, do not choose, but are carried along by forces stronger than themselves; they watch helplessly as they are crushed beneath the weight of pressures too heavy to bear. Like Beckett's characters, they are the object, not the subject, of the dramas in which they are involved. In their perplexity and confusion, they, too, suffer from a strange amnesia, wondering where they were previously and how long they have been in their present situation.[1] This bewilderment, Simenon remarks, results from an internal fissure, a rending of the inner being. Modern literature aspires to have man lose his distinguishing characteristics, to upset his chemistry, to destroy what had previously defined him, what made him what he was and what be believed he was.[2] In this process of redefinition, man has lost what had formerly been called his soul. Unable, therefore, to establish values, he is led only by vague forces; he does not initiate his actions but merely carries them out. As a result, he is not responsible for what he does, a concept that brings with it the concomitant contemporary thesis, the banality of evil. Simenon's characters murder without thought, instinctively, as they breathe. Their lack of lucidity, their subservience to blind forces, is perhaps the twentieth century "mal du siècle," more fatal than the nineteenth century despair over the divorce between ideals and reality. The type of man portrayed in Simenon's work lacks distinctive characteristics and positive values, which explains why there are no great thoughts, ambitions, or passions in Simenon's work.

Simenon's evolution as a writer has been marked by a desire to serve, "to better man's life, no matter what man, no matter what human embryo, no matter what offal."[3] He does this by demonstrating to his readers that others are prey to the same weaknesses and vices as they. What he espouses, in effect, is an acceptance of limitations, not a desire to go beyond and overcome them. His compassion for all of mankind and his understanding of the difficulty of existence, coupled with his narrative genius, account for the unprecedented popularity of his work. In reading Simenon's novels, the reader is struck by his love of life and the joys it affords. "Despite the seeming pessimism of certain of my novels," he wrote, "I am not pessimistic about life. On the contrary, I enjoy every hour of the day, every spectacle that unfolds before my eyes, every type of weather, sun or rain, snow or hail."[4] His goal, he remarks, is to give people a taste for life and for the small joys of life, for the rain as well as for a glass of beer savored on the terrace of a café.

Notes and References

(Publisher and date are indicated for Simenon's works only when the edition used differs from the one listed in the chronological bibliography.)

Preface

1. Quoted in Bernard de Fallois, *Simenon* (Paris: Gallimard, 1961), p. 260.
2. *Ibid.*, p. 263.

Chapter One

1. François Mauriac, *Le Romancier et ses personnages*, quoted in Jacques Robichon, *Mauriac* (Paris: Editions Universitaires, 1958), p. 26.
2. *Un Homme comme un autre*, p. 146.
3. André Parinaud, *Connaissance de Georges Simenon* (Paris: Presses de la Cité, 1957), p. 381.
4. *Ibid.*, p. 376.
5. *Pedigree*, pp. 12 - 13.
6. Pol Vandromme, *Georges Simenon* (Bruxelles: Pierre de Méyère, 1962), p. 15.
7. *Pedigree*, pp. 250 - 52.
8. *Je me souviens*, p. 88.
9. *Ibid.*, p. 75.
10. *Lettre à ma mère*, p. 66.
11. Jean-Jacques Tourteau, *D'Arsène Lupin à San-Antonio: Le Roman policier français de 1900 à 1970* (Tours: Mame, 1970), p. 149.
12. Marcel Moré, "Simenon et l'enfant de choeur," in F. Lacassin and G. Sigaux, eds., *Simenon* (Paris: Plon, 1973), pp. 239 - 40.
13. Parinaud, p. 407.
14. *Pedigree*, p. 19.
15. *Je me souviens*, pp. 75 - 76.
16. *Pedigree*, p. 18.
17. *Je me souviens*, pp. 65, 68.
18. *Les Quatre jours du pauvre homme* (Paris: Presses de la Cité, 1959), p. 282.
19. *Lettre à ma mère*, p. 90.
20. *Ibid.*, p. 10.
21. *Ibid.*, p. 67.

22. *Ibid.*, pp. 114 - 15.

23. *Pedigree*, p. 28.

24. *Je me souviens*, p. 33.

25. *Ibid.*, p. 43.

26. *Simenon sur le gril*, p. 15.

27. *Les Quatre jours du pauvre homme*, p. 271.

28. *Je me souviens*, p. 74.

29. *Ibid.*, p. 30.

30. *Ibid.*, p. 106.

31. *Ibid.*, p. 110.

32. Parinaud, p. 390.

33. *Simenon sur le gril*, p. 11.

34. *Je me souviens*, p. 56.

35. *Pedigree*, pp. 98 - 99.

36. *Je me souviens*, p. 215.

37. *Ibid.*, p. 89.

38. *Faubourg*, pp. 37 - 38.

39. "In 1960, 1961, 1962, for personal reasons, or for reasons I don't know myself, I began feeling old, and I began keeping notebooks. I was nearing the age of sixty." *Quand j'étais vieux*, preface, page i.

40. *Ibid.*, p. 223.

41. *Ibid.*, p. 225.

42. *Ibid.*, pp. 227 - 28.

43. *Pietr-le-Letton*, pp. 146 - 47.

44. Parinaud, p. 408.

45. *Ibid.*, p. 388.

46. *Pedigree*, p. 395.

47. Parinaud, p. 217.

48. *Pedigree*, p. 415.

49. *Ibid.*

50. *Ibid.*, p. 453.

51. *Ibid.*, p. 454.

52. *Ibid.*, p. 452.

53. *La Neige était sale* (Paris: Presses de la Cité, 1951), p. 214.

54. Brendan Gill, "Profiles: Out of the Dark," *New Yorker*, January 24, 1953, p. 35.

55. *Un Homme comme un autre*, p. 28.

56. *Les Trois crimes de mes amis* (Paris: Gallmard, 1948), p. 115.

57. "Le Romancier," p. 220.

58. *Quand j'étais vieux*, p. 52.

59. *Ibid.*, p. 53.

60. *Des traces de pas*, p. 93.

61. *Un Homme comme un autre*, pp. 312 - 13.

62. *Ibid.*, p. 68.

Chapter Two

1. *Les Mémoires de Maigret,* p. 28.
2. They were strangely linked, and often, as is evidenced in the case of Vautrin/Vidocq, they co-existed in the same person.
3. Jean-Pierre Richard, "Petites Notes sur le roman policier," *Le Français dans le monde,* 50 (juillet-août 1967), 25.
4. "I never think," p. 85. (*La Pipe de Maigret*). "I never draw conclusions", p. 117. (*Un Crime en Hollande*).
5. *Simenon sur le gril,* pp. 48 - 50.
6. *La Première enquête de Maigret,* p. 105.
7. Brigid Brophy, "Jules et Georges," *New Statesman,* LXVII, no. 1726 (April 10, 1964), 567.
8. *Le Charretier de "la Providence,"* p. 14.
9. *Ibid.,* pp. 242 - 43.
10. *Maigret se défend,* p. 10.
11. *Maigret voyage,* p. 100.
12. *M. Gallet décédé,* p. 60.
13. *Maigret et le clochard,* p. 92.
14. *Quand j'étais vieux,* p. 215.
15. *Un échec de Maigret,* p. 75.
16. *Maigret et le marchand de vin,* p. 172.
17. Thomas Narcejac, *Le Cas Simenon* (Paris: Presses de la Cité, 1950), p. 22.
18. *Maigret et le marchand de vin,* p. 211.
19. *Pietr-le-Letton,* p. 65.
20. *Maigret tend un piège. Maigret Sets a Trap* (New York: Harcourt Brace & World, 1965), pp. 170 - 71.
21. *Ibid.*
22. *Les Mémoires de Maigret,* p. 20.
23. *Ibid.,* p. 111.
24. *Pietr-le-Letton,* p. 223.
25. *New York Times,* April 2, 1974, p. 16.
26. *Simenon sur le gril,* p. 56.
27. *Ibid.,* p. 55.
28. *Quand j'étais vieux,* p. 81.
29. *Une confidence de Maigret,* pp. 15 - 16.
30. *Ibid.,* pp. 34 - 35.
31. *Maigret aux assises,* p. 78.
32. C. D. Lewis, "Chez Georges Simenon," *New York Times Book Review,* November 12, 1967, p. 48.
33. Parinaud, p. 389.
34. *Ibid.,* p. 392.
35. *Maigret et les vieillards,* p. 7.

36.   *L'Affaire Saint-Fiacre* (Paris: Fayard, 1933), pp. 50 - 51.

37.   *Ibid.*, p. 83.

38.   *Ibid.*, p. 223.

39.   *Les Mémoires de Maigret*, pp. 21 - 22.

40.   *Maigret et le clochard*, p. 137.

41.   *Des Traces de pas*, p. 157.

42.   Robert J. Courtine, one of France's leading food writers, published a book of recipes from the fictional kitchen of Madame Maigret, indicating when each dish was mentioned in one of the Maigret novels. It was translated into English under the title *Madame Maigret's Recipes* (New York: Harcourt Brace Jovanovich, 1975).

43.   Roger Stéphane, *Le Dossier Simenon* (Paris: P. Laffont, 1961), p. 61.

Chapter Three

1.   "Letter from Simenon to Gide," in Francis Lacassin and Gilbert Sigaux, eds., *Simenon*, (Paris, Plon, 1973), pp. 396 - 97.

2.   *Quand j'étais vieux*, p. 43.

3.   *Ibid.*, p. 331.

4.   *Les Demoiselles de Concarneau*, I, Edition Collective (Paris: Gallimard, 1950), p. 345.

5.   *Le Cercle des Mahé*, pp. 156 - 57, 159, 163 - 64.

6.   *Le Clan des Ostendais*, p. 11.

7.   *Ibid.*, p. 146.

8.   *Ibid.*, p. 27.

9.   *Ibid.*, p. 230.

10.   Brophy, p. 67, points out that in *Le Clan des Ostendais* a personal moral victory is set up against a whole nation's failure in morality, while the failure of Marcel, the protagonist of *Le Train*, is that of an entire nation.

11.   *Le Train*, p. 165.

12.   *Ibid.*, p. 197.

13.   *Ibid.*, p. 217.

14.   Parinaud, p. 383.

15.   *Maigret Goes to School*, in *Five Times Maigret* (New York: Harcourt Brace & World, 1964), pp. 500 - 01.

16.   *Un Nouveau dans la ville, La Mort de Belle, La Boule noire, L'Horloger d'Everton.*

17.   *Un Nouveau dans la ville*, p. 9.

18.   *Ibid.*, p. 30.

19.   Léon Thoorens, "Georges Simenon, romancier de la fuite inutile," *Revue Générale Belge*, 15 mars 1954, p. 790.

20.   *La Mort de Belle* (Paris: Presses de la Cité, 1971), pp. 144 - 45.

21.   Quoted by Eléonore Schraiber, "Georges Simenon et la littérature russe," in F. Lacassin and G. Sigaux, eds., *Simenon*, p. 187.

22. *La Boule noire*, p. 86.
23. *Ibid.*, pp. 35 - 36.
24. *Ibid.*, p. 87.
25. *Ibid.*, p. 150.
26. *Ibid.*, p. 210.
27. *Ibid.*, p. 212.
28. *Ibid.*
29. *Le Petit homme d'Arkangelsk*, p. 162.
30. *Ibid.*, p. 201.
31. *Ibid.*, pp. 162 - 63.
32. *Ibid.*, p. 211.
33. *Les Fantômes du chapelier*, p. 134.
34. *Ibid.*
35. John Raymond, *Simenon in Court* (New York: Harcourt, Brace & World, Inc., 1968), p. 91.
36. *Chez Krull*, p. 75.
37. *L'Homme de Londres* (Paris: Fayard, 1962), pp. 217 - 18.
38. *Quand j'étais vieux*, p. 162.
39. Gill, p. 41.
40. *Faubourg*, p. 166.
41. *La Veuve Couderc*, I, Edition Collective (Paris: Gallimard, 1950), pp. 72 - 73.
42. *Ibid.*, p. 55.
43. *Ibid.*, p. 96.
44. *Ibid.*, p. 167.
45. *Ibid.*
46. *Ibid.*, p. 194.
47. *Ibid.*, p. 197.
48. *L'Aîné des Ferchaux*, p. 103.
49. Anne Richter, *Georges Simenon et l'homme désintégré* (Bruxelles: La Renaissance du Livre, 1964), p. 75.
50. *Ibid.*
51. *L'Aîné des Ferchaux*, pp. 117 - 18.
52. *Ibid.*, p. 236.
53. *Ibid.*
54. *Ibid.*, p. 277.
55. Richter, p. 84.
56. *L'Aîné des Ferchaux*, pp. 298 - 99.
57. *La Neige était sale* (Paris: Presses de la Cité, 1951), p. 88.
58. *Ibid.*, pp. 95 - 96.
59. *Ibid.*, p. 122.
60. *Ibid.*
61. *Ibid.*, p. 214.
62. *Ibid.*
63. *Ibid.*, pp. 215 - 16.

64. Raymond, p. 141.
65. Narcejac, p. 125.
66. *La Neige était sale*, p. 214.
67. Narcejac, p. 66.
68. *L'Âne Rouge*, p. 182.
69. *Ibid.*, p. 205.
70. *45° à l'ombre* (Paris: Gallimard, 1963), pp. 51 - 52.
71. *Le Passager du "Polarlys,"* pp. 7 - 8.
72. *45° à l'ombre*, p. 113.
73. Interview in *Marie-France* (June 1958), quoted by Tourteau, p. 150.
74. *Le Fils*, p. 11.
75. *Ibid.*, p. 23.
76. *Ibid.*, p. 92.
77. *Le Roman de l'homme*, p. 93.
78. *Le Fils*, p. 87.
79. *Les Quatre jours du pauvre homme*, p. 400.
80. *Ibid.*, p. 405.
81. *L'Horloger d'Everton*, p. 236.
82. *Ibid.*, p. 5.
83. Richter, p. 13.
84. *L'Horloger d'Everton*, p. 72.
85. *Ibid.*, p. 137.
86. *Ibid.*, p. 191.
87. *Ibid.*, p. 238.
88. *Ibid.*, p. 246.
89. Claude Mauriac, "Georges Simenon et le secret des hommes," in *L'Alittérature contemporaine* (Paris: Editions Albin Michel, 1958), p. 147.
90. Régis Boyer, "Georges Simenon ou Nous sommes tous des assassins," II, *Le Français dans le monde*, no. 66 (juillet-août 1969), 9.

Chapter Four

1. Fallois, p. 57.
2. *Le Cercle des Mahé*, p. 164.
3. *Ibid.*, p. 217.
4. *Les Complices. The Accomplices* (New York: Harcourt, Brace & World, Inc., 1963), p. 145.
5. *Ibid.*
6. *Ibid.*, p. 256.
7. *Ibid.*, p. 284.
8. *Lettre à mon juge* (Paris: Presses de la Cité, 1951), p. 205.
9. *Ibid.*, p. 124.
10. *Ibid.*, p. 167.
11. *Ibid.*, p. 179.
12. *Ibid.*, p. 199.
13. *Ibid.*, p. 217.

14. *Ibid.*, p. 218.
15. *En cas de malheur*, p. 25.
16. *Ibid.*, pp. 138 - 39.
17. *Ibid.*, p. 141.
18. *Quand j'étais vieux*, p. 228.
19. *En cas de malheur*, p. 166.
20. *Feux rouges*, p. 9.
21. *Ibid.*, p. 16.
22. *Ibid.*, pp. 158 - 59.
23. *Ibid.*, p. 221.
24. *Antoine et Julie*, p. 87.
25. *Ibid.*, p. 155.
26. *Ibid.*, pp. 171 - 72.
27. *Ibid.*, p. 201.
28. *Ibid.*, p. 208.
29. *Ibid.*, p. 84.
30. *Ibid.*
31. *Ibid.*
32. Quoted in Léon Thoorens, *Qui êtes-vous Georges Simenon?* (Paris: Editions Géard & Cie., 1959), p. 147.
33. *Le Veuf*, p. 7.
34. *Ibid.*, p. 183.
35. *Dimanche*, p. 25.
36. *Ibid.*, p. 79.
37. *Ibid.*, pp. 141 - 42.
38. *Ibid.*, p. 168.
39. *La Main*, p. 39.
40. *Dimanche*, p. 244.
41. *La Vérité sur bébé Donge* (Paris: Gallimard, 1945), p. 187.
42. *Ibid.*, p. 218.
43. *Le Grand Bob*, p. 71.
44. *Ibid.*, p. 16.
45. *Ibid.*, p. 43.
46. *Ibid.*, p. 201.
47. *Ibid.*, pp. 179 - 80.
48. *Ibid.*, p. 180.
49. *Ibid.*
50. *Ibid.*, p. 174.
51. *Ibid.*, p. 149.
52. *Ibid.*, p. 214.
53. "The Mystery Man," interview in *Réalités*, 190 (November 1961).
54. *Trois chambres à Manhattan* (Paris: Presses de la Cité, 1951), p. 52.
55. *Ibid.*, p. 53.
56. *Ibid.*, p. 229.
57. *Ibid.*, p. 244.
58. *Ibid.*, p. 245.

59. Thoorens, p. 790.

60. *Le Voyageur de la Toussaint* (Paris: Gallimard, 1958), p. 281.

Chapter Five

1. Jacques Dubois, "Simenon et la déviance," *Littérature* (University of Paris), I (1971), 64.

2. *L'Horloger d'Everton*, p. 9.

3. *Le Passage de la ligne*, p. 50.

4. *L'Assassin*, p. 173.

5. *Lettre à mon juge*, pp. 86 - 87.

6. *Le Bourgemestre de Furnes*, p. 208.

7. *L'Homme qui regardait passer les trains*, p. 34.

8. *Ibid.*, p. 170.

9. *Ibid.*, p. 257.

10. Thoorens, p. 781.

11. Brophy, p. 67.

12. *La Fuite de Monsieur Monde* (Paris: Presses de la Cité, 1951), p. 31.

13. *Ibid.*, p. 50.

14. *Ibid.*, p. 58.

15. *Ibid.*, pp. 158 - 59.

16. *Ibid.*, p. 216.

17. *Le Bilan Malétras*, p. 80.

18. *Ibid.*, p. 176.

19. *Ibid.*, p. 213.

20. *Ibid.*, p. 221.

21. *Les Inconnus dans la maison*, 9, Edition Collective (Paris; Gallimard, 1951), pp. 366 - 67.

22. *Oncle Charles s'est enfermé* (Paris: Gallimard, 1951), p. 190.

23. *Ibid.*, p. 198.

24. François Mauriac, in F. Lacassin and G. Sigaux, eds., *Simenon*, p. 283.

25. *Les Anneaux de Bicêtre*, pp. 133 - 35.

26. *Ibid.*, p. 264.

27. *Ibid.*, pp. 226 - 28.

28. *Les Volets verts*, p. 51.

29. *Ibid.*, p. 52.

30. Parinaud, p. 383.

31. *Ibid.*

32. *Les Volets verts*, pp. 243 - 45.

33. *Ibid.*, p. 250.

34. *Ibid.*

35. *L'Enterrement de Monsieur Bouvet*, pp. 7 - 9.

36. *Ibid.*, p. 191.

37. *Ibid.*, p. 88.

38. Quoted in Parinaud, p. 390.
39. *Ibid.*
40. *L'Enterrement de Monsieur Bouvet*, pp. 220 - 21.
41. Pierre de Boisdeffre, "A la recherche de Georges Simenon," *La Revue de Paris*, 69ᵉ année, no. 9 (September 1962), p. 107.
42. Quoted by C. D. Lewis, "Chez Georges Simenon," *New York Times Book Review*, November 12, 1967, p. 4.
43. *Le Petit Saint*, p. 69.
44. *Ibid.*, pp. 21 - 22.
45. *Ibid.*, p. 118.
46. *Ibid.*, p. 199.
47. *Ibid.*, pp. 99 - 100.
48. *Ibid.*, p. 104.
49. *Ibid.*, p. 123.
50. *Ibid.*, pp. 168, 177.
51. *Ibid.*, p. 218.
52. *Ibid.*, p. 244.
53. *Ibid.*

Chapter Six

1. Vandromme, p. 53.
2. *La Mauvaise étoile* (Paris: Gallimard, 1958), p. 13.
3. *Ibid.*, p. 16.
4. *Ibid.*, p. 68.
5. *L'Heure du Nègre*, in *Oeuvres Complètes* (Lausanne: Editions Rencontre, 1967), IV, 31 - 32.
6. *Le Coup de lune*, p. 67.
7. *Ibid.*, p. 221.
8. *La Mauvaise étoile*, pp. 33 - 34.
9. *Ibid.*, p. 41.
10. *Ibid.*, p. 81.
11. *Quartier Nègre*, p. 116.
12. *Ibid.*, p. 160.
13. *Ibid.*, p. 194.
14. *Ibid.*, p. 207.
15. *La Mauvaise étoile*, pp. 57 - 58.
16. *Le Testament Donadieu* (Paris: Gallimard, 1960), p. 318.
17. *Touriste de bananes*, p. 39.
18. *Ibid.*, p. 174.
19. *Ibid.*, p. 217.
20. *La Mauvaise étoile*, pp. 145 - 46.
21. *Le Blanc à lunettes*, p. 150.
22. *Sous peine de mort*, in Lindsay and Nazzaro, eds. *Trois Nouvelles* (New York: Appleton Century Crofts, 1966), p. 101.
23. *Ibid.*, p. 107.

24. *Ibid.*, p. 117.
25. *Ibid.*, p. 128.
26. *Ibid.*, p. 140.
27. *Ibid.*, pp. 140 - 41.

Chapter Seven

1. *Le Roman de l'homme*, pp. 22 - 23.
2. *Ibid.*, p. 92.
3. Carvel Collins, "The Art of Fiction IX: Georges Simenon," *The Paris Review*, 9 (Summer 1955), 75.
4. Parinaud, p. 395.
5. *Les Trois crimes de mes amis* (Paris: Gallimard, 1948), pp. 11 - 12.
6. *Le Bourgemestre de Furnes*, p. 226.
7. *Maigret et son mort*, p. 181.
8. *Le Cercle des Mahé*, p. 42.
9. *Ibid.*, p. 22.
10. The same image is used in *Les Anneaux de Bicêtre*.
11. *Mon ami Maigret*, in *Oeuvres Complètes*, XIV, 133.
12. Stéphane, p. 119.
13. *Le Bourgemestre de Furnes*, p. 93.
14. *Le Cercle des Mahé*, pp. 15, 18.
15. Stéphane, p. 110.
16. *L'Heure du Nègre*, p. 14.
17. *La Jument perdue*, p. 11.
18. *Le Fond de la bouteille*, pp. 28 - 29.
19. *Les Frères Rico*, p. 10.
20. *Les Témoins récalcitrants*, p. 9.
21. *Un Echec de Maigret*, pp. 9 - 10.
22. *Les Scrupules de Maigret*, p. 9.
23. *Maigret et le clochard*, pp. 9 - 10.
24. *Maigret et l'homme tout seul*, pp. 11 - 12.
25. George Steiner, *Language and Silence* (New York: Atheneum, 1967), p. 211.
26. *La Mort d'Auguste*, pp. 129 - 30.
27. Parinaud, p. 395.
28. *La Mort d'Auguste*, p. 89.
29. *Ibid.*, pp. 125 - 26.
30. *Ibid.*, pp. 80 - 81.
31. *Ibid.*, p. 126.
32. *Ibid.*, pp. 242-43.
33. *Ibid.*, p. 244.
34. Preface to *Traqué* by Arthur Omré, in Lacassin and Sigaux, eds., *Simenon*, p. 371.
35. Parinaud, p. 414.

36. "The Mystery Man," interview in *Réalités*, 190 (November 1961), 26.

37. "Le Romancier," *French Review*, XIX, no. 4 (February 1946), 228.

38. Henry Anatole Grunwald, "The World's Most Prolific Novelist," *Life*, 45 (November 3, 1958), 96.

39. Parinaud, p. 400.

40. Grunwald, p. 96.

41. Quoted by Collins, p. 78.

42. *Ibid.*, pp. 78 - 79.

43. *Le Président,* pp. 217 - 19.

44. Raymond, p. 22.

Chapter Eight

1. See Samuel Beckett, *Waiting for Godot* (New York: Grove Press, 1954).

2. Quoted in Richter, p. 6.

3. *Quand j'étais vieux*, p. 32.

4. *Un Homme comme un autre*, p. 22.

Selected Bibliography

(Includes only works published under Simenon's name. Simenon's complete works have been published since 1967 under the direction of Gilbert Sigaux by Editions Rencontre, Lausanne, in seventy-two volumes. One series numbered in Roman numerals from I to XXVIII contains the Maigret novels and all of the detective short stories. The other series, numbered in Arabic from 1 to 44, contains the other novels, articles, essays, and autobiographical works.)

PRIMARY SOURCES

1. Maigret Novels and Short Stories

Pietr-le-Letton. Paris: Fayard, 1931. *Maigret and the Enigmatic Lett.* Harmondsworth, Middlesex: Penguin Books, 1963.

M. Gallet décédé. Paris: Fayard, 1931. *Maigret Stonewalled.* Baltimore: Penguin, 1963.

Le Pendu de Saint-Pholien. Paris: Fayard, 1931. *Maigret and the Hundred Gibbets.* Harmondsworth, Middlesex: Penguin, 1963.

Le Charretier de "la Providence." Paris: Fayard, 1931. *Maigret Meets a Milord.* Harmondsworth, Middlesex: Penguin, 1963.

La Tête d'un homme. Paris: Fayard, 1931. In *The Patience of Maigret.* New York: Harcourt Brace & Co., 1940.

Le Chien jaune. Paris: Fayard, 1931. In *The Patience of Maigret.* New York: Harcourt Brace & Co., 1940.

La Nuit du Carrefour. Paris: Fayard, 1931. *Maigret at the Crossroads.* Baltimore: Penguin, 1964.

Un Crime en Hollande. Paris: Fayard, 1931. *A Crime in Holland.* In *Maigret Abroad.* New York: Harcourt Brace & Co., 1940.

Au rendez-vous des Terre-Neuvas. Paris: Fayard, 1931. *The Sailors' Rendez-vous.* Harmondsworth, Middlesex: Penguin, 1970.

La Danseuse du Gai-Moulin. Paris: Fayard, 1931. *At the "Gai-Moulin."* In *Maigret Abroad.* New York: Harcourt Brace & Co., 1940.

La Guingette à deux sous. Paris: Fayard, 1931. *The Guingette by the Seine.* In *Maigret to the Rescue.* London: Routledge, 1940.

Le Port des brumes. Paris: Fayard, 1932. *Death of a Harbor Master.* In *Maigret and M. Labbe.* New York: Harcourt Brace & Co., 1942.

L'Ombre chinoise. Paris: Fayard, 1932. *Maigret Mystified.* Harmondsworth, Middlesex: Penguin, 1964.

L'Affaire Saint-Fiacre. Paris: Fayard, 1932. *Maigret Goes Home.* Baltimore: Penguin, 1967.

153

Chez les Flamands. Paris: Fayard, 1932. *The Flemish Shop.* In *Maigret to the Rescue.* London: Routledge, 1940.

Le Fou de Bergerac. Paris: Fayard, 1932. *Le Fou de Bergerac.* In *Maigret Travels South.* London: Routledge, 1940.

Liberty-Bar. Paris: Fayard, 1932. *Liberty-Bar.* In *Maigret Travels South.* London: Routledge, 1940.

L'Ecluse no. 1. Paris: Fayard, 1933. *The Lock at Charenton.* In *Maigret Sits it Out.* London: Routledge, 1941.

Maigret. Paris: Fayard, 1934. *Maigret Returns.* In *Maigret Sits it Out.* London: Routledge, 1941.

Les Nouvelles enquêtes de Maigret. Paris; Gallimard, 1944. *The Short Cases of Inspector Maigret.* New York: Doubleday, 1959.

Cécile est morte. In *Maigret revient.* Paris: Gallimard, 1942.

Les Caves du Majestic. In *Maigret revient.* Paris: Gallimard, 1942.

La Maison du juge. In *Maigret revient.* Paris: Gallimard, 1942.

Signé Picpus. Paris: Gallimard, 1944. *To Any Lengths.* Harmondsworth, Middlesex: Penguin, 1958.

L'Inspecteur cadavre. In *Signé Picpus.* Paris: Gallimard, 1944.

Félicie est là. In *Signé Picpus.* Paris: Gallimard, 1944.

La Pipe de Maigret. Paris: Presses de la Cité, 1947.

Maigret se fâche. In *La Pipe de Maigret.* Paris: Presses de la Cité, 1947.

Maigret à New York. Paris: Presses de la Cité, 1947. *Inspector Maigret in New York's Underworld.* New York: New American Library, 1956.

Maigret et l'inspecteur malchanceux. Paris: Presses de la Cité, 1947.

Les Vacances de Maigret. Paris: Presses de la Cité, 1948. *No Vacation for Maigret.* New York: Bantam Books, 1959.

Maigret et son mort. Paris: Presses de la Cité, 1948. *Maigret's Special Murder.* London: Hamilton, 1964.

La Première enquête de Maigret (1913). Paris: Presses de la Cité, 1949. *Maigret's First Case.* London: Heinemann Educational Publishers, 1970.

Mon ami Maigret. Paris: Presses de la Cité, 1949. *My Friend Maigret.* In *Maigret Triumphant.* London: Hamilton, 1969.

Maigret chez le coroner. Paris: Presses de la Cité, 1949.

Maigret et la vieille dame. Paris: Presses de la Cité, 1950. *Maigret and the Old Lady.* In *Maigret Cinq.* New York: Harcourt, Brace & World, 1965.

L'Amie de Mme Maigret. Paris: Presses de la Cité, 1950. *Madame Maigret's Friend.* London: Hamilton, 1960.

Un Noël de Maigret. Paris: Presses de la Cité, 1951.

Les Mémoires de Maigret. Paris: Presses de la Cité, 1951. *Maigret's Memoirs.* London: Hamilton, 1963.

Maigret au Picratt's. Paris: Presses de la Cité, 1951. *Maigret in Montmartre.* Harmondsworth, Middlesex: Penguin, 1963.

Maigret en meublé. Paris: Presses de la Cité, 1951. *Maigret Takes a Room.* In *Maigret Cinq.* New York: Harcourt, Brace & World, 1965.

Maigret et la grande perche. Paris: Presses de la Cité, 1951. *Maigret and the Burglar's Wife*. In *Maigret Triumphant*. London: Hamilton, 1969.

Maigret, Lognon et les gangsters. Paris: Presses de la Cité, 1952. *Maigret and the Gangsters*. London; Hamilton, 1974.

Le Revolver de Maigret. Paris: Presses de la Cité, 1952. *Maigret's Revolver*. In *Maigret Triumphant*. London: Hamilton, 1969.

Maigret et l'homme du banc. Paris: Presses de la Cité, 1953. *Maigret and the Man on the Bench*. New York: Harcourt Brace Jovanovich, 1975.

Maigret a peur. Paris: Presses de la Cité, 1953. *Maigret Afraid*. London: Hamilton, 1961.

Maigret se trompe. Paris: Presses de la Cité, 1953. *Maigret's Mistake*. In *Five Times Maigret*. New York: Harcourt, Brace & World, 1964.

Maigret à l'école. Paris: Presses de la Cité, 1954. *Maigret Goes to School*. In *Five Times Maigret*. New York: Harcourt, Brace & World, 1964.

Maigret et la jeune morte. Paris: Presses de la Cité, 1964. *Maigret and the Dead Girl*. In *Maigret Cinq*. New York: Harcourt, Brace & World, 1965.

Maigret chez le ministre. Paris: Presses de la Cité, 1955. *Maigret and the Calame Report*. New York: Harcourt, Brace & World, 1969.

Maigret et le corps sans tête. Paris: Presses de la Cité, 1955. *Maigret and the Headless Corpse*. London: Hamilton, 1967.

Maigret tend un piège. Paris: Presses de la Cité, 1955. *Maigret Sets a Trap*. London: Hamilton, 1965.

Un échec de Maigret. Paris: Presses de la Cité, 1957. *Maigret's Failure*. London: Hamilton, 1962.

Maigret s'amuse. Paris: Presses de la Cité, 1957. *Maigret's Little Joke*. In *Maigret Cinq*. New York: Harcourt, Brace & World, 1965.

Maigret voyage. Paris: Presses de la Cité, 1957. *Maigret and the Millionaires*. New York: Harcourt Brace Jovanovich, 1974.

Les Scrupules de Maigret. Paris: Presses de la Cité, 1957. *Maigret Has Scruples*. London: Hamilton, 1959.

Maigret et les témoins récalcitrants. Paris: Presses de la Cité, 1959. *Maigret and the Reluctant Witnesses*. In *Five Times Maigret*. New York: Harcourt, Brace & World, 1964.

Une Confidence de Maigret. Paris: Presses de la Cité, 1959. *Maigret Has Doubts*. London: Hamilton, 1968.

Maigret aux assises. Paris: Presses de la Cité, 1960. *Maigret in Court*. London: Hamilton, 1961.

Maigret et les vieillards. Paris: Presses de la Cité, 1960. *Maigret in Society*. London: Hamilton, 1962.

Maigret et le voleur paresseux. Paris: Presses de la Cité, 1961. *Maigret and the Lazy Burglar*. London: Hamilton, 1963.

Maigret et les braves gens. Paris: Presses de la Cité, 1962. *Maigret and the Black Sheep*. New York: Harcourt Brace Jovanovich, 1976.

Maigret et le client du samedi. Paris: Presses de la Cité, 1962. *Maigret and the Saturday Caller.* London: Hamilton, 1964.

Maigret et le clochard. Paris: Presses de la Cité, 1963. *Maigret and the Bum.* New York: Harcourt Brace Jovanovich, 1973.

La Colère de Maigret. Paris: Presses de la Cité, 1963. *Maigret Loses His Temper.* Harmondsworth: Penguin Books, 1967.

Maigret et le fantôme. Paris: Presses de la Cité, 1964. *Maigret and the Apparition.* New York: Harcourt Brace Jovanovich, 1975.

Maigret se défend. Paris: Presses de la Cité, 1964. *Maigret on the Defensive.* Harmondsworth: Penguin Books, 1968.

La Patience de Maigret. Paris: Presses de la Cité, 1965. *The Patience of Maigret.* London: Hamilton, 1966.

Maigret et l'affaire Nahour. Paris: Presses de la Cité, 1966. *Maigret and the Nahour Case.* London: Hamilton, 1967.

Le Voleur de Maigret. Paris: Presses de la Cité, 1967. *Maigret's Pickpocket.* London: Hamilton, 1968.

Maigret à Vichy. Paris: Presses de la Cité, 1968. *Maigret in Vichy.* New York: Harcourt Brace & World, 1969.

Maigret hésite. Paris: Presses de la Cité, 1968. *Maigret Hesitates.* New York: Harcourt Brace & World, 1970.

L'Ami d'enfance de Maigret. Paris: Presses de la Cité, 1968. *Maigret's Boyhood Friend.* New York: Harcourt Brace & World, 1970.

Maigret et le tueur. Paris: Presses de la Cité, 1969. *Maigret and the Killer.* New York: Harcourt Brace Jovanovich, 1971.

Maigret et le marchand de vin. Paris: Presses de la Cité, 1970. *Maigret and the Wine Merchant.* New York: Harcourt Brace Jovanovich, 1971.

La Folle de Maigret. Paris: Presses de la Cité, 1970. *Maigret and the Madwoman.* New York: Harcourt Brace Jovanovich, 1972.

Maigret et l'homme tout seul. Paris: Presses de la Cité, 1971. *Maigret and the Loner.* New York: Harcourt Brace Jovanovich, 1975.

Maigret et l'indicateur. Paris: Presses de la Cité, 1971. *Maigret and the Informer.* New York: Harcourt Brace Jovanovich, 1973.

Maigret et Monsieur Charles. Paris: Presses de la Cité, 1972. *Maigret and M. Charles.* London: Hamilton, 1973.

2. Novels

Le Relais d'Alsace. Paris: Fayard, 1931. *The Man from Everywhere.* In *Maigret and M. Labbe.* New York: Harcourt Brace & Co., 1942.

Le Passager du "Polarlys." Paris; Fayard, 1932. *Danger at Sea.* In *On Land and Sea.* New York: Hanover House, 1954.

Les Gens d'en face. Paris: Fayard, 1933. *The Window Over the Way.* Baltimore: Penguin, 1966.

L'Âne Rouge. Paris: Fayard, 1933.

La Maison du canal. Paris: Fayard, 1933. *House by the Canal.* London: Routledge, 1948.

Les Fiançailles de M. Hire. Paris: Fayard, 1933. *M. Hire's Engagement.* In
     The Sacrifice. London: Hamilton, 1956.
Le Coup de lune. Paris: Fayard, 1933. *Tropic Moon.* In *In Two Latitudes.*
     London: Routledge, 1942.
Le Haut Mal. Paris: Fayard, 1933. *The Woman in the Grey House.* In *Af-
     fairs of Destiny.* New York: Harcourt Brace & Co., 1944.
L'Homme de Londres. Paris: Fayard, 1933. *Newhaven-Dieppe.* In *Affairs
     of Destiny.* New York: Harcourt Brace & Co., 1944.
Le Locataire. Paris: Gallimard, 1934. *The Lodger.* In *Escape in Vain.* Lon-
     don: Routledge, 1943.
Les Suicidés. Paris: Gallimard, 1934. *One Way Out.* In *Escape in Vain.*
     London: Routledge, 1943.
Les Pitard. Paris: Gallimard, 1935. *A Wife at Sea.* London: Routledge &
     Kegan Paul, 1949.
Les Clients d'Avrenos. Paris: Gallimard, 1935.
Quartier Nègre. Paris: Gallimard, 1935.
Les Demoiselles de Concarneau. Paris: Gallimard, 1936. *The Breton Sisters.*
     In *Havoc by Accident.* London: Routledge, 1943.
45° à l'ombre. Paris: Gallimard, 1936.
Long Cours. Paris: Gallimard, 1936.
L'Evadé. Paris: Gallimard, 1936.
Faubourg. Paris: Gallimard, 1937. *Home Town.* In *On The Danger Line.*
     New York: Harcourt Brace & Co., 1944.
L'Assassin. Paris: Gallimard, 1937. *The Murderer.* Harmondsworth:
     Penguin, 1963.
Le Blanc à lunettes. Paris: Gallimard, 1937. *Talatala.* In *Havoc by Acci-
     dent.* New York: Harcourt Brace & Co., 1943.
Le Testamant Donadieu. Paris: Gallimard, 1937. *The Shadow Falls.* Lon-
     don: Routledge, 1945.
Ceux de la Soif. Paris: Gallimard, 1938.
Chemin sans issue. Paris: Gallimard, 1938. *Blind Alley.* New York: Har-
     court Brace & Co., 1946.
L'Homme qui regardait passer les trains. Paris: Gallimard, 1938. *The Man
     Who Watched the Trains Go By.* New York: Berkeley Publishing
     Co., 1958.
Les Rescapés du "Télémaque." Paris: Gallimard, 1938. *The Survivors.* In
     Black Rain. Harmondsworth: Penguin, 1965.
Monsieur la Souris. Paris: Gallimard, 1938. *The Mouse.* Harmondsworth:
     Penguin, 1966.
Touriste de bananes ou les Dimanches de Tahiti. Paris: Gallimard, 1938.
     Banana Tourist. In *Lost Moorings.* London: Routledge, 1946.
La Marie du Port. Paris: Gallimard, 1938.
Le Suspect: Paris: Gallimard, 1938. *The Green Thermos.* In *On the Danger
     Line.* London: Routledge, 1944.

Les Soeurs Lacroix. Paris: Gallimard, 1938.

Le Cheval Blanc. Paris: Gallimard, 1938.

Chez Krull. Paris: Gallimard, 1939. *Chez Krull.* London: New English Library, 1966.

Le Bourgemestre de Furnes. Paris: Gallimard, 1939. *Burgomaster of Furnes.* London: Routledge, 1952.

Le Coup de vague. Paris: Gallimard, 1939.

Les Inconnus dans la maison. Paris: Gallimard, 1940. *Strangers in the House.* New York: Doubleday, 1954.

Malempin. Paris: Gallimard, 1940.

Cour d'assises. Paris: Gallimard, 1941.

La Maison des sept jeunes filles. Paris: Gallimard, 1941.

L'Outlaw. Paris: Gallimard, 1941.

Bergelon. Paris: Gallimard, 1941.

Il pleut bergère. . . . Paris: Gallimard, 1941. *Black Rain.* Harmondsworth, Middlesex: Penguin, 1965.

Le Voyageur de la Toussaint. Paris: Gallimard, 1941. *Strange Inheritance.* London: Pan Books, 1958.

Oncle Charles s'est enfermé. Paris: Gallimard, 1942.

Le Veuve Couderc. Paris: Gallimard, 1942. *The Widow.* New York: Doubleday, 1955.

La Vérité sur bébé Donge. Paris: Gallimard, 1942. *I Take This Woman.* In *Satan's Children.* New York: Prentice-Hall, 1953.

Le Fils Cardinaud. Paris: Gallimard, 1942. *Young Cardinaud.* In *The Sacrifice.* London: Hamilton, 1956.

Le Rapport du gendarme. Paris: Gallimard, 1944. *The Gendarme's Report.* London: Routledge, 1951.

La Fenêtre des Rouet. Paris: Editions de la Jeune Parque, 1945. *Across the Street.* London: Routledge, 1954.

L'Aîné des Ferchaux. Paris: Gallimard, 1945. *Magnet of Doom.* London: Routledge, 1948.

Les Noces de Poitiers. Paris: Gallimard, 1946.

Le Cercle des Mahé. Paris: Gallimard, 1946.

La Fuite de Monsieur Monde. Paris: Editions de la Jeune Parque, 1947. *M. Monde Vanishes.* London: Hamilton, 1967.

Trois Chambres à Manhattan. Paris: Presses de la Cité, 1947. *Three Beds in Manhattan.* New York: Doubleday, 1964.

Au bout du rouleau. Paris: Presses de la Cité, 1947.

Le Clan des Ostendais. Paris: Gallimard, 1947. *The Ostenders.* London: Routledge, 1952.

Lettre à mon juge. Paris: Presses de la Cité, 1947. *Act of Passion.* New York: Prentice-Hall, 1952.

Le Destin des Malou. Paris: Presses de la Cité, 1947. *The Fate of the Malous.* London: Hamilton, 1962.

Le Passager clandestin. Paris: Editions de la Jeune Parque, 1947. *The Stowaway.* London: Hamilton, 1957.

Pedigree. Paris: Presses de la Cité, 1948. *Pedigree*. New York: London House, 1963.

Le Bilan Malétras. Paris: Gallimard, 1948.

La Jument perdue. Paris: Presses de la Cité, 1948.

La Neige était sale. Paris: Presses de la Cité, 1948. *Stain on the Snow*. Baltimore: Penguin, 1964.

Le Fond de la bouteille. Paris: Presses de la Cité, 1949. *The Bottom of the Bottle*. In *Tidal Wave*. New York: Doubleday, 1954.

Les Fantômes du chapelier. Paris: Presses de la Cité, 1949. *The Hatter's Ghost*. London: Hamilton, 1956.

Les Quatre jours du pauvre homme. Paris: Presses de la Cité, 1949. *Four Days in a Lifetime*. In *Satan's Children*. New York: Prentice-Hall, 1953.

Un Nouveau dans la ville. Paris: Presses de la Cité, 1950.

Les Volets verts. Paris: Presses de la Cité, 1950. *The Heart of a Man*. New York: Prentice-Hall, 1951.

L'Enterrement de Monsieur Bouvet. Paris: Presses de la Cité, 1950. *The Burial of Monsieur Bouvet*. In *Destinations*. New York: Doubleday, 1955.

Tante Jeanne. Paris: Presses de la Cité, 1951. *Aunt Jeanne*. London: Routledge, 1953.

Le Temps d'Anaïs. Paris: Presses de la Cité, 1951. *The Girl in His Past*. New York: Prentice-Hall, 1952.

Une Vie comme neuve. Paris: Presses de la Cité, 1951. *A New Lease on Life*. New York: Doubleday, 1963.

Marie qui louche. Paris: Presses de la Cité, 1952.

La Mort de Belle. Paris: Presses de la Cité, 1952. *Belle*. In *An American Omnibus*. New York: Harcourt Brace and World, 1967.

Les Frères Rico. Paris: Presses de la Cité, 1952. *The Brothers Rico*. In *An American Omnibus*. New York: Harcourt Brace and World, 1967.

Antoine et Julie. Paris: Presses de la Cité, 1953. *The Magician*. New York: Doubleday, 1955.

L'Escalier de fer. Paris: Presses de la Cité, 1953. *The Iron Staircase*. London: H. Hamilton, 1963.

Feux rouges. Paris: Presses de la Cité, 1953. *The Hitchhiker*. In *An American Omnibus*. New York: Harcourt Brace and World, 1967.

Crime impuni. Paris: Presses de la Cité, 1954. *The Fugitive*. New York: Doubleday, 1955.

L'Horloger d'Everton. Paris: Presses de la Cité, 1954. *The Watchmaker of Everton*. In *An American Omnibus*. New York: Harcourt Brace and World, 1967.

Le Grand Bob. Paris: Presses de la Cité, 1955. *Big Bob*. In *Fifth Simenon Omnibus*. Harmondsworth, Middlesex: Penguin, 1972.

Les Témoins. Paris: Presses de la Cité, 1955. *The Witnesses*. New York: Doubleday, 1956.

La Boule noire. Paris: Presses de la Cité, 1955.

Les Complices. Paris: Presses de la Cité, 1956. *The Accomplices*. New York: Harcourt Brace and World, 1963.

En cas de malheur. Paris: Presses de la Cité, 1956. *In Case of Emergency*. New York: Doubleday, 1958.

Le Petit homme d'Arkangelsk. Paris: Presses de la Cité, 1956. *The Little Man from Archangel*. New York: Harcourt Brace and World, 1966.

Le Fils. Paris: Presses de la Cité, 1957. *The Son*. London: H. Hamilton, 1958.

Le Nègre. Paris: Presses de la Cité, 1957. *The Negro*. London: Hamilton, 1959.

Strip-tease. Paris: Presses de la Cité, 1958. *Strip-tease*. London: Hamilton, 1959.

Le Président. Paris: Presses de la Cité, 1958. *The Premier*. New York: Harcourt Brace and World, 1966.

Le Passage de la ligne. Paris: Presses de la Cité, 1958.

Dimanche. Paris: Presses de la Cité, 1958. *Sunday*. New York: Harcourt Brace and World, 1966.

La Vieille. Paris: Presses de la Cité, 1959.

Le Veuf. Paris: Presses de la Cité, 1959. *The Widower*. London: Hamilton, 1961.

L'Ours en peluche. Paris: Presses de la Cité, 1960. *Teddy Bear*. New York: Harcourt Brace Jovanovich, 1972.

Betty. Paris: Presses de la Cité, 1961. *Betty*. New York: Harcourt Brace Jovanovich, 1975.

Le Train. Paris: Presses de la Cité, 1961. *The Train*. New York: Harcourt Brace and World, 1966.

La Porte. Paris: Presses de la Cité, 1962. *The Door*. London: Hamilton, 1964.

Les Autres. Paris: Presses de la Cité, 1962. *The House on the Quai Notre-Dame*. New York: Harcourt Brace Jovanovich, 1975.

Les Anneaux de Bicêtre. Paris: Presses de la Cité, 1963. *The Bells of Bicêtre*. New York: Harcourt Brace and World, 1964.

La Chambre bleue. Paris: Presses de la Cité, 1964. *The Blue Room*. New York: Harcourt Brace and World, 1964.

L'Homme au petit chien. Paris: Presses de la Cité, 1964. *The Man With the Little Dog*. London: Hamilton, 1965.

Le Petit Saint. Paris: Presses de la Cité, 1965. *The Little Saint*. New York: Harcourt Brace and World, 1965.

Le Train de Venise. Paris: Presses de la Cité, 1965. *The Venice Train*. New York: Harcourt Brace Jovanovich, 1974.

Le Confessionnal. Paris: Presses de la Cité, 1966. *The Confessional*. New York: Harcourt Brace and World, 1968.

La Mort d'Auguste. Paris: Presses de la Cité, 1966. *The Old Man Dies*. New York: Harcourt Brace and World, 1967.

Le Chat. Paris: Presses de la Cité, 1967. *The Cat.* New York: Harcourt Brace and World, 1967.

Le Déménagement. Paris: Presses de la Cité, 1967. *The Move.* New York: Harcourt Brace and World, 1968.

La Prison. Paris: Presses de la Cité, 1968. *The Prison.* New York: Harcourt Brace and World, 1969.

La Main. Paris: Presses de la Cité, 1968. *The Man on the Bench in the Barn.* New York: Harcourt Brace and World, 1970.

Il y a encore des noisetiers. Paris: Presses de la Cité, 1969.

Novembre. Paris: Presses de la Cité, 1969. *November.* New York: Harcourt Brace Jovanovich, 1970.

Le Riche homme. Paris: Presses de la Cité, 1970. *The Rich Man.* New York: Harcourt Brace Jovanovich, 1971.

La Disparition d'Odile. Paris: Presses de la Cité, 1971. *The Disappearance of Odile.* London: Hamilton, 1972.

La Cage de verre. Paris: Presses de la Cité, 1971. *The Glass Cage.* London: Hamilton, 1973.

Les Innocents. Paris: Presses de la Cité, 1972. *The Innocents.* New York: Harcourt Brace Jovanovich, 1973.

3. Short Stories
(Most of these short stories appeared in various newspapers and magazines. Only bound collections are listed. All of them are included in the *Oeuvres Complètes.*)

La Folle d'Itteville. Paris: Haumont, 1931.

Les Treize mystères. Paris: Fayard, 1932.

Les Treize énigmes. Paris: Fayard, 1932.

Les Treize coupables. Paris: Fayard, 1932.

Les Sept minutes. Paris: Gallimard, 1938.

Le Petit Docteur. Paris: Gallimard, 1943.

Les dossiers de l'Agence O. Paris: Gallimard, 1943.

Nouvelles exotiques. Paris: Gallimard, 1944.

Les Petits Cochons sans queue. Paris: Presses de la Cité, 1949.

Le Bateau d'Emile. Paris: Gallimard, 1954.

La Rue aux Trois Poussins. Paris: Presses de la Cité, 1963.

4. Autobiographical Works

Les Trois crimes de mes amis. Paris: Gallimard, 1938.

La Mauvaise étoile. Paris: Gallimard, 1938.

"L'Aventure." In *Les Etincelles.* Lyon: Editions de Savoie, 1945.

"L'Age du roman." In Special number 21 - 24 of magazine *Confluences.* Lyon: 1943.

Je me souviens. Paris: Presses de la Cité, 1945.

"Le Romancier." *The French Review,* XIX, no. 4 (February 1946), pp. 212 - 29.

Le Roman de l'homme. Speech delivered at Brussels World's Fair, October
3, 1958. Paris: Presses de la Cité, 1960. *The Novel of Man.* New
York: Harcourt Brace and World, 1964.
Quand j'étais vieux. Paris: Presses de la Cité, 1970. *When I Was Old.* New
York: Harcourt Brace Jovanovich, 1971.
Lettre à ma mère. Paris: Presses de la Cité, 1974. *Letter to My Mother.*
New York: Harcourt Brace Jovanovich, 1976.
Des Traces de pas. Paris: Presses de la Cité, 1975.
Un Homme comme un autre. Paris: Presses de la Cité, 1975.
Les Petits hommes. Paris: Presses de la Cité, 1976.
Vent du nord-Vent du sud. Paris: Presses de la Cité, 1976.

SECONDARY SOURCES

(The following is a partial list of selected secondary sources.)
AUSTIN, RICHARD. "Simenon's Maigret and Adler." *International Review*,
340 - 342 (1970), 45 - 50. Also in Francis Lacassin and Gilbert Sigaux,
eds., *Simenon*, 197 - 203. Paris: Plon, 1973. Compares Simenon's
view of life with that of psychologist Adler, but makes serious error
when he states that for Simenon, as for Adler, man is master of his
fate.
BOILEAU-NARCEJAC. *Le Roman Policier.* Paris: Payot, 1964. Study of
Simenon's detective novels within the context of detective novels in
general.
BOISDEFFRE, PIERRE DE. "A la recherche de Simenon." *La Revue de Paris*,
69ᵉ année, no. 9 (September 1962), 96 - 107.
————. "Le Secret de Georges Simenon." *La Revue de Paris*, 65ᵉ année,
no. 1 (January 1958), 173 - 74. Simenon and modern themes of guilt,
expatriation, and solitude.
BOYER, RÉGIS. "Georges Simenon ou Nous sommes tous des assassins." *Le
Français dans le monde*, 64 (April-May 1969), 13 - 17; 66 (July-
August 1969), 9 - 15. Excellent study emphasizing Simenon's thesis
that all men are capable of murder if driven to their limit.
BRONNE, CARLO. "Simenon académicien." *La Revue des Deux Mondes*,
10 (May 15, 1952), 272 - 82. Speech by historian Carlo Bronne
welcoming Simenon to membership in the Académie Royale de
langue et de littérature.
BROPHY, BRIGID. "Jules et Georges." *New Statesman*, LXVII, no. 1726
(April 10, 1964), 566, 568. Study of *Le Train*.
COLLINS, CARVEL. "The Art of Fiction IX: Georges Simenon." *The Paris
Review*, 9 (Summer 1955), 71 - 90. Excellent interview with Simenon
on his technique and ideas.
DESONAY, FERNAND. "Georges Simenon, romancier et académicien." *Le
Flambeau*, 35e année, no. 2 (1953); continued in no. 3, 251 - 62.
Biographical details, analysis, and study of *Les Trois crimes de mes
amis* and several Maigrets.

DUBOIS, JACQUES. "Simenon et la déviance." *Littérature*, I (1971), 62 - 72. One of the best studies of Simenon's work. It analyzes six novels that deal with the theme of deviance from the norm. The deviant, in sociological terms, is one who transgresses the norms of the group to which he belongs and thus provokes hostile reactions on the part of the majority of the group.

DUBOURG, MAURICE. "Petite Géographie de Simenon." *La Fenêtre ouverte*, 43 (December 1950), 7 - 30. Also in Francis Lacassin and Gilbert Sigaux, eds., *Simenon*, 139 - 56. Paris: Plon, 1973. Traces varied geographical backgrounds of Simenon's novels.

FALLOIS, BERNARD DE. *Simenon*. Paris: Gallimard, 1961. Rev. ed., Lausanne: Editions Rencontre, 1971. Outstanding study of Simenon's work and the best in Simenon's opinion. Also contains biographical section, anthology, selected criticism, bibliography, interview with Parinaud.

FRANCK, FREDERICK. *Simenon's Paris*. New York: The Dial Press, 1970. Beautiful nostalgic collection of Franck's illustrations of Paris accompanied by appropriate texts from Simenon's works.

GILL, BRENDAN. "Profiles: Out of the Dark." *New Yorker*, January 24, 1953, pp. 35 - 45. Valuable study of Simenon's career until 1953.

GILLOIS, ANDRÉ. *Qui êtes-vous Georges Simenon?* Paris: Gallimard, 1953. Interview.

GRUNWALD, HENRY ANATOLE. "World's Most Prolific Novelist." *Life*, 45 (November 3, 1958), 95 - 96. Analysis of creation of Simenon's novels.

JOUR, JEAN. *Simenon et "Pedigree."* Liége: Editions de l'essai, 1963. A bit too dependent on Parinaud. Explains all of Simenon's work based on *Pedigree*.

LACASSIN, FRANCIS and SIGAUX, GILBERT, eds. *Simenon*. Paris: Plon, 1973. Collected essays and studies of Simenon's work by prominent critics including the editors, selected texts by Simenon, selections from correspondence between Simenon and André Gide, bibliography. Excellent.

MAURIAC, CLAUDE. "Georges Simenon et le secret des hommes." In *L'Alittérature contemporaine*. Paris: Albin Michel, 1958. Emphasis on metaphysical aspects of Simenon's work, the contemporary themes of guilt and alienation.

MORÉ, MARCEL. "Simenon et l'enfant de choeur." *Dieu Vivant*, 19 (1951), 39 - 69. Reprinted in Francis Lacassin and Gilbert Sigaux, eds., *Simenon*, pp. 227 - 63. Paris: Plon, 1973. Stresses importance of Simenon's early Catholic formation on his work.

NARCEJAC, THOMAS. *Le Cas Simenon*. Paris: Presses de la Cité, 1950. Study of Simenon's techniques, themes, atmosphere, his view of humanity. Excellent.

NORD, PIERRE. "Le Roman dans l'histoire: de l'Odyssée, au récit d'aventures moderne." *Les Annales*, Nouvelle série no. 227 (September

1969), 3 - 19. Role of adventure novel, both detective and spy, in
literature.

PARINAUD, ANDRÉ. *Connaissance de Georges Simenon*. Paris: Presses de la
Cité. 1957. Places writer and work within his period. Excellent
analysis of *Pedigree* and relationship of Simenon's life to his work,
followed by an interview on Simenon's ideas and methods originally
broadcast over the radio in October and November 1955.

POULET, ROBERT. *La Lanterne magique*. Paris: Debresse, 1956. Contains
two articles on Simenon's gift of observation limited to second rate,
mediocre individuals.

RADINE, SERGE. *Quelques aspects du roman policier psychologique*.
Geneva: Editions du Mont-Blanc, 1960. Discusses Simenon as a
moralist in the tradition of classic novel of psychological analysis.

RAYMOND, JOHN. *Simenon in Court*. New York: Harcourt Brace and
World, 1968. The only book length study of Simenon's work in
English prior to the present volume. Excellent analysis of Simenon's
work.

RICHARD, JEAN-PIERRE. "Petites Notes sur le roman policier." *Le Français
dans le monde*, 50 (July-August 1967), 23 - 28. Excellent historical
study of the detective novel.

RICHTER, ANNE. *Georges Simenon et l'homme désintégré*. Bruxelles: La
Renaissance du Livre, 1964. Excellent study of modern faceless man
in Simenon's work.

RITZEN, QUENTIN. *Simenon Avocat des hommes*. Paris: Le Livre Contem-
porain, 1961. Analyzes Simenon's work in terms of Simenon as
spokesman for Everyman.

ROLO, CHARLES J. "Simenon and Spillane: The Metaphysics of Murder
for the Millions." In *New World Writing*, pp. 234 - 45. New York:
The New American Library of World Literature, 1952. Excellent
study of the mystery story and the problem of evil, how it provides
reader with a hero who answers profound needs. It is modern man's
passion play.

Simenon sur le gril. Paris: Presses de la Cité, 1968. Simenon interviewed
by five doctors.

STÉPHANE, ROGER. *Le Dossier Simenon*. Paris: P. Laffont, 1961. Particularly good in study of sensuality and imagery.

THOORENS. LÉON. "Georges Simenon, romancier de la fuite inutile."
Revue Générale Belge, 90e année (March 15, 1954), 781 - 98. Studies
several of Simenon's novels to demonstrate that all of Simenon's
heroes are rebels, unaware that flight is useless because it is impossible to escape your destiny.

TOURTEAU, JEAN-JACQUES. *D'Arsène Lupin à San-Antonio: Le Roman
policier français de 1900 à 1970*. Tours: Mame, 1970. Study of
methods and techniques used by French authors of detective novels

and of espionage from 1900 - 1969. Section on Simenon provides keys to his work.

TREMBLAY, N. J. "Simenon's Psychological Westerns." *Arizona Quarterly*, 3 (Autumn 1954), 217 - 26. Analysis of *La Jument perdue* and *Le Fond de la bouteille*.

VALLIÈRES, PIERRETTE. "Simenon et le néo-réalisme." *Paris-Théâtre*, 9ᵉ année, no. 101 (October 1955), 6 - 9. Simenon's cinematographic techniques.

VANDROMME, POL. *Georges Simenon*. Bruxelles: Pierre de Méyère, 1962.

―――――. "Simenon ou le style de l'humanité moyenne." *Défense de l'occident*, 21 (March-April 1962), 43 - 52. Study of disintegration of Simenon's heroes, their lack of comprehension of the forces that destroy them.

Index